AF690265

The Snippet Handbook: Reusable Code for Beginners

By

Susie Hala

Copyright Page

For permissions, inquiries, or bulk purchases, please contact:
Hala Learning Press
Email: **info@youraistudybuddy.com**

ISBN: 979-8-9991963
Printed in the United States of America

Author: **Susie Hala**

Disclaimer

This publication is designed to provide educational information about coding concepts, software development, and the use of reusable code snippets. The material is provided *"as is"* and is not intended to serve as professional, technical, legal, or financial advice.

While every effort has been made to ensure accuracy, the author and publisher make no representations or warranties regarding the completeness, reliability, or suitability of the information or code samples contained herein. Readers should use their professional judgment and verify results before implementing any examples in real-world environments.

By using the information in this book, you agree that **Susie Hala, Hala Learning Press, and all affiliates shall not be held liable** for any direct, indirect, incidental, or consequential damages resulting from the application or misuse of the material presented.

All trademarks, logos, and brand names mentioned are the property of their respective owners. References to third-party tools, software, or services are for educational illustration only and do not constitute endorsement.

Author's Rights & AI Assistance Notice

TABLE OF CONTENTS

The Snippet Handbook: Reusable Code for Beginners

💥 *THE 28-DAY AI PROMPT MASTERY CHALLENGE*

Created by Susie Hala, Author of "What to Say When You Talk to AI"

Learn the 4 C's of AI Communication: Clarity, Context, Creativity, and Consistency

In 28 days, you'll explore the world's leading AI tools — mastering how to communicate, create, and collaborate with intelligence that listens, learns, and responds to you.

🧠 WEEK 1 – THE ART OF CONTEXT

(Teach AI to Think Like You)

Day 1 – Claude
Create a personalized "AI coach" who knows your goals and tone.

Day 2 – Perplexity
Ask a deep research question using layers of context — who, what, and why.

Day 3 – Canva Magic
Design an infographic with your AI book quote as the central theme.

Day 4 – Gemini
Generate a weekly planner using clear context about your routines.

Day 5 – Otter.ai
Record a short thought and have AI summarize your main idea.

Day 6 – ElevenLabs
Clone your voice or read your words aloud — test emotional accuracy.

Day 7 – Reflection
What did you learn about "feeding context" to get smarter answers?

🎨 WEEK 2 – CREATIVITY WITHOUT LIMITS

(Let AI Imagine With You)

Day 8 – Midjourney
Turn a single descriptive sentence into a powerful visual story.

Day 9 – ChatGPT
Co-write a 100-word poem that blends technology and humanity.

Day 10 – Runway ML
Make a 10-second video that brings one of your AI ideas to life.

Day 11 – DALL·E 3
Illustrate a book scene using detailed, artistic prompts.

Day 12 – Headspace AI
Compose a calming affirmation script using kind, creative tone.

Day 13 – Pictory
Convert a paragraph into a cinematic video reel.

Day 14 – Reflection
Which tool made you feel most creative or inspired?

✍ WEEK 3 – CLARITY IS POWER

(Get AI to Understand You Instantly)

Day 15 – Notion AI
Design a "Clarity Tracker" template for goal-setting.

Day 16 – Jasper AI
Write a 3-sentence product pitch using short, strong verbs.

Day 17 – GrammarlyGO
Edit your prompts for precision, grammar, and tone.

Day 18 – Zapier
Automate a workflow using clear step-by-step instructions.

Day 19 – QuillBot
Refine an unclear paragraph into something crisp and confident.

Day 20 – Rewind
Review your past AI prompts and highlight unclear wording.

Day 21 – Reflection
Write down 3 "rules of clarity" that improve every AI prompt you write.

🔁 WEEK 4 – CONSISTENCY BUILDS TRUST

(Train AI to Mirror Your Voice and Style)

Day 22 – Loom
Record a 60-second message to explain one AI concept your way.

Day 23 – Brain.fm
Use AI-generated focus music while writing your daily prompt.

Day 24 – Wysa
Create a gentle, encouraging conversation with AI.

Day 25 – Krisp
Polish your video or audio with background noise removed.

Day 26 – Miro AI
Map your long-term AI learning goals visually.

Day 27 – Brancher.ai
Build a mini "Prompt Idea Generator" app with your favorite examples.

Day 28 – Gamma.app
Design a presentation showcasing your AI journey through the 4 C's.

🖤 YOUR MISSION

By the end of 28 days, you'll:
✅ Master the *language of clarity* when talking to AI.
✅ Use *context* to make AI your creative partner.
✅ Harness *creativity* to inspire fresh ideas.
✅ Build *consistency* to keep your unique voice across every AI tool.

🎓 Join the Challenge!

👉 Visit **YourAIStudyBuddy.com** to download your printable tracker, reflection sheets, and certificate of completion.
💬 Share your journey using **#4CsAIChallenge** and tag **@YourAIStudyBuddy**

📌 Quick Reference Guide

For Writing: ChatGPT, Claude, GrammarlyGO, CopyAI, Copilot
For Research: Perplexity AI, Elicit, Gemini, Techpresso
For Visuals: Midjourney, Firefly
For Video: Sora
For Audio: ElevenLabs, Voicemod, Suno AI
For Automation: Manus AI, AgentGPT
For Developers: Llama 3, DeepSeek
For Conversation: ChatGPT, Claude, Gemini, Grok

💡 How to Use This Guide

Choose by Task:

- Need to write content? Start with ChatGPT or Claude
- Need visuals? Go to Midjourney or Firefly
- Need research? Use Perplexity AI or Elicit

Choose by Skill Level:

- **Beginners:** ChatGPT, Gemini, GrammarlyGO, Midjourney
- **Intermediate:** Claude, Perplexity AI, Copilot, ElevenLabs
- **Advanced:** AgentGPT, Llama 3, DeepSeek

Choose by Integration:

- **Google Workspace:** Gemini 2.5 Pro
- **Microsoft Office:** Copilot
- **Creative Cloud:** Firefly

All tools listed are as of October 2025. Features, pricing, and availability may change. Visit each tool's official website for the most current information.

The Bit and Byte Family

Definition and Overview

The **Bit and Byte Family** forms the digital DNA of every computer system — the foundation upon which all programming, AI models, and data storage are built.
A **bit** (short for *binary digit*) is the smallest possible unit of digital information. It can hold one of two values: **0 or 1**, representing *off/on* or *false/true*.
When multiple bits are grouped together, they form **bytes**, **kilobytes**, **megabytes**, and beyond — a structured hierarchy that allows machines to represent everything from numbers and letters to photos, videos, and artificial intelligence models.

In simple terms:

Bits are like individual letters.
Bytes are like words.
Larger data units are like sentences, paragraphs, and books that computers can read.

This binary language is the silent conversation between humans and machines — the bridge between electrical signals and digital understanding. Every AI model, every chat, every image, and even every word in this book is made possible by this family of data units.

⚙️ Why It Matters in AI and Prompt Engineering

When you communicate with an AI model, you're indirectly working with billions — sometimes trillions — of bits and bytes.

- Your *prompts* are converted into numerical representations (tokens), which are sequences of bits.
- The *AI's responses* are computed, stored, and transmitted as bytes.
- Even *model weights* — the learned "memory" of an AI — are measured in gigabytes or terabytes.

Understanding this family helps readers appreciate how language is converted into electrical patterns and stored as data inside vast neural architectures.

🧠 Key Insight for Readers

Think of the Bit and Byte Family as the **alphabet of machines**.
If prompt engineering is the art of speaking to AI, then bits and bytes are the *sound waves* that carry your words to the machine's ears.

The Bit and Byte Family Tree

Member	Abbreviation	Size (Approx.)	Meaning / Example	Used For
Bit	b	1 binary value	Smallest unit of data (0 or 1)	Representing logical states (true/false, on/off)
Nibble	—	4 bits	Half a byte (rarely used term but important)	Hexadecimal representation (0–F)

Member	Abbreviation	Size (Approx.)	Meaning / Example	Used For
Byte	B	8 bits	Smallest addressable unit in memory	Storing a single character (e.g., "A")
Kilobyte	KB	1,024 bytes	About one paragraph of text	Small files, metadata
Megabyte	MB	1,024 KB	About a short book	Images, documents
Gigabyte	GB	1,024 MB	Around 230 songs or 2 hours of HD video	Software, model weights
Terabyte	TB	1,024 GB	Roughly 500 hours of movies	Data storage drives, training datasets
Petabyte	PB	1,024 TB	Massive data collections	AI training corpora, research archives
Exabyte	EB	1,024 PB	Global-scale digital data	Internet traffic, cloud storage
Zettabyte	ZB	1,024 EB	Almost the entire global digital footprint	Global data analytics, cloud AI systems
Yottabyte	YB	1,024 ZB	Theoretical maximum — beyond current storage	Future large-scale AI and quantum data

Analogy for Everyday Readers

If you think of information as water:

- A **bit** is a single drop.
- A **byte** is a spoonful.
- A **megabyte** is a glass.
- A **terabyte** is a swimming pool.
- A **yottabyte** is an entire ocean of digital information.

Each level represents a deeper scale of capacity — and in AI, these digital oceans are where our models *learn, think, and evolve.*

Quick Takeaway

Every AI thought begins as a single bit — and every masterpiece of machine intelligence is built from countless bytes working in harmony.

The Qubit Family

Definition and Overview

The **Qubit Family** (short for *quantum bit*) represents the next generation of digital intelligence — a revolutionary leap from the classical *bit*.
While a bit can exist only as a **0 or 1**, a **qubit** can exist as **both 0 and 1 at the same time**,

thanks to the quantum principle of **superposition**.
This unique property allows quantum computers to perform multiple calculations simultaneously, processing vast combinations of data at once — a feat impossible for traditional systems.

In other words:

If bits are switches that can be "on" or "off," qubits are *waves* that can be "on," "off," or anything in between — all at the same moment.

Quantum computing redefines how we process, store, and use information. For AI and prompt engineering, it hints at a future where machine reasoning could become exponentially faster, more complex, and more energy-efficient.

Why It Matters in AI and Prompt Engineering

Large language models (LLMs) and AI systems today run on classical computers powered by bits and bytes. But researchers are already developing **quantum-enhanced models** that could dramatically increase computational speed and reduce training costs.
Qubits open the door to:

- Faster optimization and simulation in AI algorithms
- Exponentially larger search spaces for data analysis
- Quantum-based encryption and security models
- Quantum machine learning (QML) — blending neural networks with quantum mechanics

When this technology matures, the relationship between **prompts, probabilities, and reasoning** will evolve again — allowing AI to explore infinite possibilities simultaneously instead of one outcome at a time.

Key Insight for Readers

Think of qubits as the **dreamers of the digital world** — able to hold contradictions, possibilities, and probabilities in balance.
Prompt engineers of tomorrow will likely need to think *quantumly* — phrasing requests that account for parallel reasoning and multi-dimensional responses.

The Qubit Family Tree

Member	Symbol / Abbreviation	Quantum Concept	Explanation	Used For
Qubit	`	ψ⟩`	**Superposition**	Can represent both 0 and 1 simultaneously

Member	Symbol / Abbreviation	Quantum Concept	Explanation	Used For
Entangled Qubits	—	**Entanglement**	Two or more qubits linked so that one's state instantly affects the other	Secure communication, teleportation
Quantum Register	—	**State Vector**	A collection of qubits storing multi-dimensional data	Quantum computing memory
Quantum Gate	`H, X, Y, Z`	**Quantum Logic Operation**	Manipulates qubits (like logic gates in classical computing)	Quantum algorithms and processing
Quantum Circuit	—	**Quantum Flow**	A sequence of gates that performs a specific computation	Quantum algorithm design
Quantum Superposition	—	**Wave Property**	A qubit existing in multiple states simultaneously	Parallel processing of data
Quantum Entanglement	—	**Linked States**	Correlation between qubits, even at distance	Quantum communication and AI synchronization
Quantum Decoherence	—	**Loss of Quantum State**	When qubits lose their quantum behavior due to noise	Main limitation in today's systems
Quantum Error Correction	—	**Stability Control**	Protects information from decoherence	Reliable quantum computing
Quantum Measurement	—	**State Collapse**	Converts the probabilistic state into a definite outcome	Producing readable results

🌍 Analogy for Everyday Readers

If **bits** are like *flat paint colors*, each showing one tone at a time,
then **qubits** are *rainbows in motion* — blending all colors until you decide to look.
Only when measured (or "observed") does a qubit choose a single color — just as reality chooses one outcome from infinite possibilities.

💬 Quick Takeaway

The Qubit Family turns computing from logic into possibility — from "yes or no" to "maybe all at once."
This is the foundation for the coming age of **quantum artificial intelligence.**

⚡ The Watts Family

Definition and Overview

The **Watts Family** represents the energy backbone of the digital universe.
A **watt (W)** is a unit of power — the rate at which energy is consumed or converted. In computing, every process that runs, every bit that flips, and every prompt you submit consumes electrical energy measured in watts.

When multiple watts are measured over time, they become **watt-hours (Wh)**, **kilowatt-hours (kWh)**, or **megawatt-hours (MWh)** — the same units that appear on your electricity bill. From powering your laptop to running massive AI data centers, the Watts Family governs the invisible current that brings artificial intelligence to life.

⚙ Why Energy Matters to AI

AI doesn't just think — it *consumes*.
Every AI model requires energy for **training, storage, and inference** (the process of responding to prompts).
For example:

- Training a large model like GPT or Gemini can require energy equivalent to powering **hundreds of homes for a year**.
- Every prompt response you receive from an AI runs on GPUs (graphics processing units) that draw **hundreds to thousands of watts per second**.
- The world's biggest data centers, where these models live, are designed with energy optimization in mind — cooling, redundancy, and renewable energy integration.

Energy efficiency is now one of the **core frontiers of AI innovation.**
Companies and researchers aim to reduce carbon footprints through hardware design (like NVIDIA's energy-optimized GPUs), software efficiency (fewer parameters, better algorithms), and renewable power sourcing.

In essence, *energy is the heartbeat of intelligence.*
Without watts, even the smartest AI is silent.

🧠 Key Insight for Readers

Every prompt you send — every "conversation" with AI — triggers a real, physical reaction somewhere in the world.
Transistors switch, GPUs heat, fans spin, and electrons race through circuits.
That process costs energy, measured in watts, which converts electrical potential into computational intelligence.

The future of AI depends not just on smarter algorithms, but on **smarter energy management.**
Efficiency, sustainability, and innovation all begin with the Watts Family.

⚡ The Watts Family Tree

Member	Symbol / Abbreviation	Measurement	Explanation	Used In
Watt	`W`	1 Joule per second	The base unit of power	CPUs, GPUs, servers
Kilowatt	`kW`	1,000 Watts	Power scale for small systems	Desktops, local servers
Megawatt	`MW`	1,000 kW	Used for large data centers	AI data clusters
Gigawatt	`GW`	1,000 MW	City-level power output	Regional AI hubs
Watt-Hour	`Wh`	Power over time	Measures energy consumption	Battery usage
Kilowatt-Hour	`kWh`	1,000 Wh	Common billing unit	Energy tracking and optimization
Joule	`J`	1 Newton meter	Physical unit of energy	Thermodynamics, hardware physics
Calorie (small)	`cal`	4.184 Joules	Heat energy equivalent	Energy-to-heat conversion
Thermal Watt	—	—	Heat dissipated by hardware	Cooling and thermal systems
Efficiency Ratio	—	Output/Input (unitless)	Measures how much energy becomes useful work	AI energy optimization

🌑 Analogy for Everyday Readers

If information is *the brain* of AI, then **energy is its blood**.
Watts are what keep every digital neuron alive — from your phone's processor to the world's largest AI supercomputers.
No matter how intelligent a model becomes, without energy, it can't think, create, or respond.

💬 Quick Takeaway

The Watts Family fuels every AI breakthrough.
Intelligence without energy is potential; energy without control is waste.
The future belongs to technologies that learn to balance both.

What Is an LLM?

A **Large Language Model (LLM)** is an advanced type of artificial intelligence trained to understand, interpret, and generate human-style language.
Instead of memorizing facts, it learns by studying enormous collections of text—books,

websites, articles, and digital conversations—to discover how words, ideas, and patterns connect.

At the heart of most LLMs is a **transformer architecture**, a deep neural network that processes many words at once and learns which ones influence each other. Through this structure, the model becomes capable of predicting the next word in a sentence, completing thoughts, or even creating entirely new text that sounds natural and context-aware.

What makes LLMs "large" is their **scale**—they contain billions or even trillions of parameters (the digital "neurons" that store learned knowledge). These parameters enable the model to perform countless language-based tasks, such as writing essays, generating computer code, summarizing information, answering questions, or translating text across languages.

However, an LLM doesn't truly *understand* meaning the way humans do. It predicts responses based on probability and patterns learned during training.
That's why your **prompts**—the instructions you give—are so important. The clearer and more intentional your wording, the more accurate, creative, and insightful the AI's replies will be.

This book will teach you how to communicate effectively with LLMs—to guide their reasoning, reduce errors, and unlock their full creative potential.

Human-Style Language

Definition:

Human-style language refers to the natural, expressive way people communicate — using tone, emotion, rhythm, and context that sound authentic to everyday conversation.
When an AI model speaks or writes in "human style," it produces responses that feel **warm, relatable, and conversational**, rather than mechanical or robotic.

Key Characteristics

1. **Natural Flow:**
   Words and sentences follow the same rhythm and structure that people use when speaking or writing casually.
   Example:
   - Human-style: *"That's a great idea! Let's see how we can make it work."*
   - Robotic-style: *"Acknowledged. Idea is feasible. Proceeding to analyze."*
2. **Tone and Emotion:**
   It reflects mood — friendly, serious, professional, or empathetic — depending on the context of the conversation.
3. **Context Awareness:**
   The AI understands *how* something is said, not just *what* is said.
   It adjusts its wording based on the user's personality, topic, and goal.
4. **Personal Connection:**
   Uses pronouns ("you," "we," "I"), metaphors, and examples to sound more human and engaging.

5. **Adaptive Communication:**
   The AI can shift tone — casual, formal, educational, persuasive — just like a human speaker would in different situations.

Why It Matters in AI Communication

Human-style language helps bridge the gap between **technology and trust.**
When AI responds naturally, users feel understood, respected, and comfortable continuing the conversation.
It transforms AI from a tool into a **partner** — one that listens, empathizes, and communicates effectively.

In short:

"Human-style language makes AI sound like it's talking *with* you, not *at* you."

Example in AI Prompting

Prompt:

"Explain quantum computing in human-style language."

AI Response:

"Imagine a computer that doesn't just pick one answer at a time but explores many possibilities all at once — that's what quantum computing does."

✅ The explanation uses **everyday imagery**, **simple words**, and **a friendly tone** — hallmarks of human-style communication.

Applications

- **Customer Service Bots** that sound caring and helpful.
- **AI Tutors** that explain complex ideas in simple, human terms.
- **Writing Assistants** that produce conversational marketing or blog content.
- **AI Agents** (like the ones you're building for YourAIStudyBuddy.com) that teach or guide with empathy and clarity.

Summary

Human-style language is the art of making AI sound less like a computer and more like a companion.
It uses tone, empathy, and understanding to connect naturally with people.
In prompting, asking AI to "respond in human-style language" ensures the output feels authentic, easy to read, and emotionally intelligent.

Transformer Architecture

Definition:

The **Transformer architecture** is a deep learning model introduced in 2017 by Vaswani et al. in the paper *"Attention Is All You Need."*
It revolutionized artificial intelligence by enabling models to understand and generate human language more efficiently than ever before.
Transformers are now the backbone of large language models (LLMs) such as **ChatGPT, BERT, Gemini, Claude, and GPT-4.**

Key Concept: Attention Mechanism

At the heart of the Transformer is a system called **self-attention**, which allows the model to focus on the most important words in a sentence — regardless of their position.
Instead of reading text word-by-word like older models, Transformers process the entire sequence at once and learn **which words influence each other most strongly.**

Example:
In the sentence *"The cat sat on the mat because it was tired,"*
the Transformer knows that "it" refers to "the cat," not "the mat."
It learns this by assigning higher **attention weights** between related words.

Key Components

1. **Encoder:**
    - Reads and processes the input text.
    - Breaks the text into tokens and builds representations (embeddings).
    - Each encoder layer uses **self-attention** and **feed-forward networks** to understand relationships.
2. **Decoder:**
    - Generates output (for example, a translation or response).
    - Uses both **self-attention** (to understand its own generated words) and **cross-attention** (to relate them to the input).
3. **Positional Encoding:**
    - Since Transformers don't read sequentially like RNNs, positional encodings tell the model *where* each word appears in a sentence.
4. **Multi-Head Attention:**
    - The model uses several attention "heads" to look at relationships from multiple perspectives at once (syntax, meaning, emotion, etc.).
5. **Feed-Forward Layers:**
    - After attention, each layer passes data through small neural networks that refine and strengthen understanding.

Benefits

✅ **Parallel Processing:**
Processes all words at once instead of one at a time — much faster.

✅ **Better Context Understanding:**
Recognizes long-range dependencies between words in large texts.

✅ **Scalable:**
Can be trained on massive datasets for translation, summarization, question answering, and chatbots.

✅ **Transfer Learning:**
Pretrained models can be fine-tuned for new tasks with smaller datasets.

Disadvantages

⚠ **Resource Intensive:**
Requires huge amounts of memory and computing power.

⚠ **Black-Box Problem:**
Difficult to fully interpret how attention weights lead to specific outputs.

⚠ **Bias Retention:**
Can inherit biases from the training data.

Applications

- **Language Translation** (Google Translate)
- **Text Generation** (ChatGPT, Bard, Claude)
- **Summarization & Question Answering**
- **Speech Recognition and Image Captioning**
- **Code Generation** (GitHub Copilot, Replit Ghostwriter)

Analogy

A Transformer works like a team of readers highlighting a document.
Each reader focuses on different key words and phrases, then they combine their insights to produce a complete, context-aware understanding.

Summary

The **Transformer architecture** changed the field of AI forever.
It introduced a smarter, faster way for machines to understand human language using **attention** instead of repetition.
Because of this breakthrough, today's AI systems can write essays, translate speech, create art, and hold meaningful conversations.

🧠 Breaking Down the Transformer Architecture

Definition (In Simple Terms):

The **Transformer Architecture** is a framework that helps AI models understand and generate language.
It's built like a two-part machine — an **encoder** that reads information and a **decoder** that writes or predicts what comes next.
Its secret power comes from something called **"attention"** — the ability to focus on the most important parts of a sentence or context, just like how humans pay attention when listening or reading.

1. The Core Idea: "Attention Is All You Need"

Before Transformers, older models like RNNs (Recurrent Neural Networks) read text one word at a time, which was slow and hard for long sentences.
Transformers changed everything by allowing the model to **look at all words at once** and decide which ones matter most — this is called **self-attention**.

Example:
In the sentence:

"The cat sat on the mat because it was tired."
The Transformer learns that **"it"** refers to **"the cat,"** not the mat.
It "pays attention" to the right relationship automatically.

2. The Two Main Parts

A. Encoder – The Reader

The **encoder** takes in the input text (your question, sentence, or paragraph) and converts it into numbers the AI can understand (called **embeddings**).

Each encoder layer performs two main jobs:

1. **Self-Attention:** Finds relationships between words.
2. **Feed-Forward Layer:** Refines those relationships mathematically to build meaning.

Encoders are stacked — often 6 to 12 layers deep — to build rich understanding.

B. Decoder – The Writer

The **decoder** uses what the encoder learned and generates an output — word by word — predicting what comes next.

Each decoder layer also performs two jobs:

1. **Self-Attention (on the output so far):** Understands what it has already generated.
2. **Cross-Attention:** Connects its generated text back to the encoded input for accuracy.

That's how AI can take a prompt like:

"Write a story about a robot learning kindness,"
and output a complete story that stays on topic and emotionally consistent.

3. How the Transformer Works — Step by Step

Here's the process in simple stages:

Step	What Happens	Example in Human Terms
1 Input	Text is split into tokens (words/pieces).	Like breaking a sentence into puzzle pieces.
2 Embedding	Tokens are converted into vectors (numbers).	Giving each word its "meaning code."
3 Positional Encoding	Adds information about word order.	Knowing "dog bites man" ≠ "man bites dog."
4 Attention	Model finds relationships between words.	Decides which words relate most strongly.
5 Feed-Forward	Data passes through small neural layers.	Refines understanding of meaning.
6 Output	Decoder predicts next words or sentences.	Writes, translates, or answers clearly.

4. Key Components (In Simple Language)

Component	Purpose	Analogy
Self-Attention	Helps AI focus on important words in context.	Like highlighting key ideas in a paragraph.
Multi-Head Attention	Looks at multiple meanings or patterns at once.	Like several readers focusing on different parts of the same story.
Positional Encoding	Reminds the AI of word order.	Like giving each word its address in a sentence.
Feed-Forward Network	Adds depth and refinement.	Like summarizing what you learned from reading.
Normalization	Keeps data balanced and stable.	Like editing your thoughts before speaking.
Softmax Layer	Chooses the most likely next word.	Like picking the best answer out of many options.

5. Why Transformers Changed Everything

✅ **Speed:**
They process all words simultaneously, not one by one.

✅ **Context Understanding:**
They remember long-range relationships (for example, "he" in paragraph three referring to "John" in paragraph one).

✅ **Scalability:**
They can grow in size (GPT-3, GPT-4, Claude, etc.) without losing performance.

✅ **Adaptability:**
They can handle text, images, audio, and even video — all using similar architecture.

6. Real-World Examples

AI Model	Built On Transformer?	Purpose
BERT (Google)	✅ Yes	Understanding sentence meaning for search.
GPT Series (OpenAI)	✅ Yes	Generating human-like text and conversations.
T5 (Google)	✅ Yes	Translating, summarizing, and text rewriting.
Vision Transformers (ViT)	✅ Yes	Understanding images like a human brain.

7. Summary (In Human Style)

The **Transformer Architecture** is like a powerful translator between human language and machine understanding.
It reads everything at once, pays attention to what matters, and learns relationships that give meaning to text.

Because of Transformers, AI can now:

- Write books.
- Translate languages.
- Create music.
- Understand emotion and context.

It's the reason why when you talk to AI today — it sounds natural, intelligent, and human-like.

Diagram: How the Transformer Architecture Works

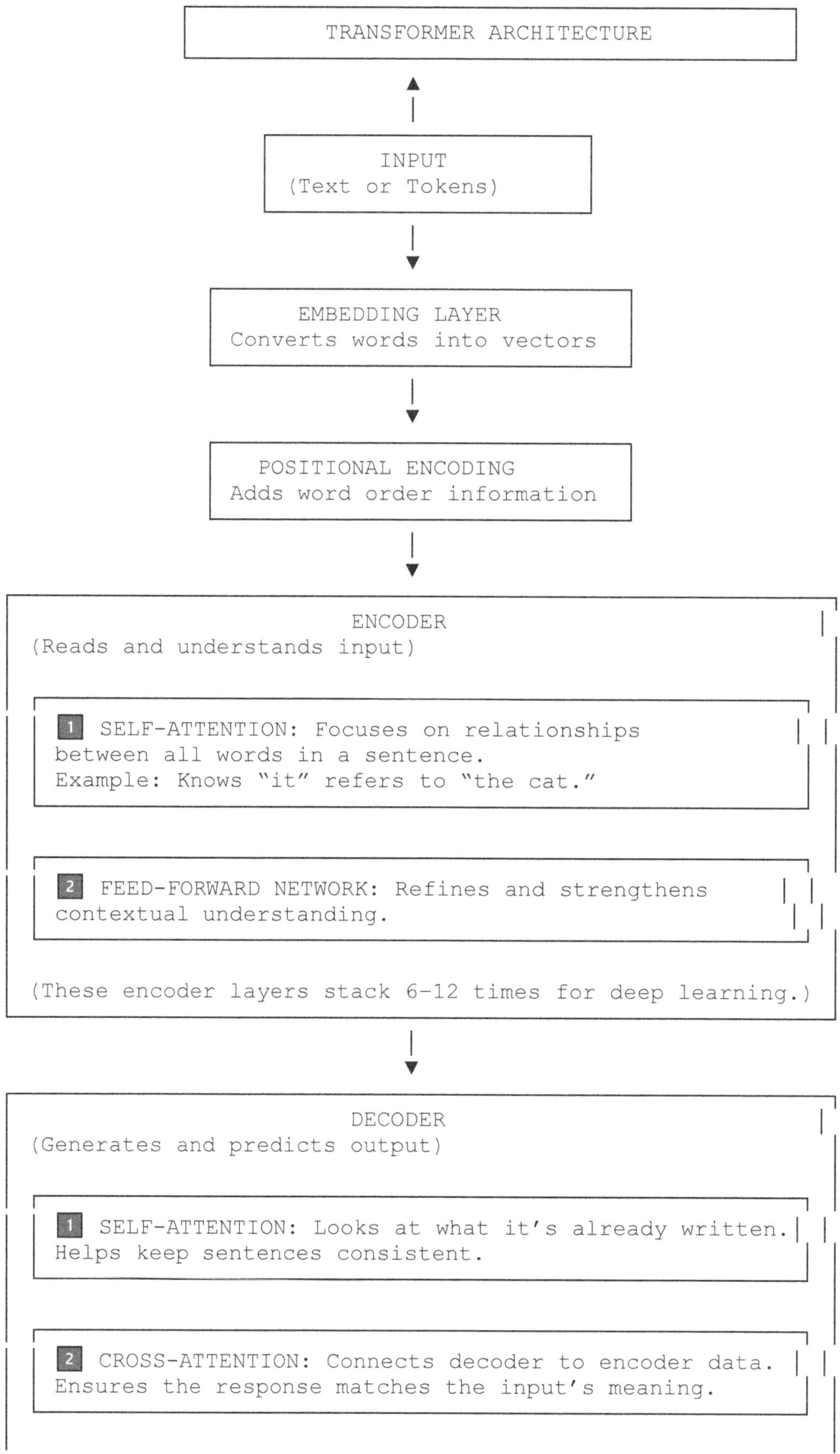

```
│ ┌──────────────────────────────────────────────────────┐ │
│ │ 3️⃣ FEED-FORWARD LAYERS: Final refinement and output. │ │
│ └──────────────────────────────────────────────────────┘ │
└──────────────────────────────────────────────────────────┘
                              │
                              ▼
                 ┌─────────────────────────────┐
                 │           OUTPUT            │
                 │ (Predicted words, text, etc.)│
                 └─────────────────────────────┘
```

🧩 Simple Flow Summary

Step	What Happens	Purpose
1️⃣	Input text is broken into tokens.	Prepares words for processing.
2️⃣	Embeddings + positional encoding applied.	Adds meaning and order.
3️⃣	Encoder analyzes and builds understanding.	Learns context and relationships.
4️⃣	Decoder generates new words step by step.	Produces sentences or translations.
5️⃣	Output becomes the final human-style text.	You see the answer or completion.

💡 Quick Analogy

The Transformer works like a skilled translator team:
One side (Encoder) *reads and understands everything*,
the other side (Decoder) *writes and speaks fluently* —
and both communicate through attention to make sure every idea stays connected.

Figure 11.2 – How the Attention Mechanism Works in a Transformer

Diagram: The Attention Mechanism Explained

```
ATTENTION MECHANISM (Simplified)

        ▲
        |

Input Sentence
"The cat sat on the mat
 because it was tired."

        |
        ▼

Step 1: Tokenization
Each word is split and given an ID.
[The] [cat] [sat] [on] [the] [mat] [because]
[it] [was] [tired]

        |
        ▼

Step 2: Embedding
Words are converted into numeric vectors
(representing meaning, not just spelling).

        |
        ▼

Step 3: Self-Attention
The model looks at ALL words at once
and decides which ones are related.

        |
        ▼

Example Focus:
When analyzing the word "it," the AI
gives highest attention weight to "cat" –
because "it" refers to "the cat."

        |
        ▼

Step 4: Attention Weights
Numbers (0.0 to 1.0) show connection strength
Example:
 "it" → "cat" = 0.95 (strong link)
 "it" → "mat" = 0.15 (weak link)

        |
        ▼

Step 5: Weighted Context
Each word is re-represented with weighted
meanings – forming a rich understanding
of the entire sentence.

        |
        ▼

Step 6: Output
The AI now "understands" the relationships
```

```
and can predict or generate accurate text.
```

🧩 In Simple Words

Attention is how AI learns to *focus* — it doesn't treat every word equally.
Instead, it gives **more weight** to the words that matter most for meaning.

💡 Analogy

Think of attention like reading comprehension:
When you read a sentence, your brain automatically highlights the important words that give context to the rest.
The Transformer does the same — it *pays attention* to what's relevant and ignores what's not.

📊 Key Benefit

This mechanism allows the AI to:

- Understand long sentences easily.
- Keep context even in large paragraphs.
- Translate meaning across languages.
- Sound more *human-style* and context-aware in its replies.

Top 10 LLMs (2025) — Notable Models to Know

Below is a snapshot of some of the most influential and capable LLMs today. Use this as a reference in your prompt experiments and comparative thinking.

#	Model	Highlights / Use Cases
1	**GPT-4.5 / GPT Series (OpenAI)**	The flagship series behind ChatGPT, strong in reasoning, writing, and tool integration.
2	**Claude (Anthropic)**	Known for alignment and safe responses, with versions like Claude 3.7 and Claude 4.
3	**Gemini (Google)**	Multimodal (text, image, audio), long-context capability, integrated into Google services. Zapier+1
4	**LLaMA (Meta)**	Meta's open / community-friendly family of models; increasingly powerful in each release. Instaclustr+2TechTarget+2
5	**Mistral**	Strong open-source contender, good balance between performance and resource cost. Klu+1
6	**DeepSeek-V3**	Emerging model with high capability in math, code, and reasoning. Splunk+2Codingscape+2
7	**Falcon**	Open model strong in speed and efficiency, used for many real-world applications. TechTarget+1

#	Model	Highlights / Use Cases
8	**Grok (xAI)**	Launched by Elon Musk's xAI; designed for conversational and reasoning tasks.
9	**Qwen (Alibaba / Open Source)**	Good multilingual and instruction-tuned model; strong in code and reasoning. KDnuggets+1
10	**Nemotron / Other Experimental / Future Models**	Cutting-edge architectures often in research or limited release, worth watching as the field develops.

Note: This list is illustrative and may evolve as new models appear or existing ones improve. Always test with your own prompts and goals.

🔠 The Token Family

Definition and Overview

The **Token Family** represents the language currency of artificial intelligence — the smallest readable unit of meaning that an AI model understands.
Just as humans read words and sentences, large language models (LLMs) process **tokens**.
A *token* can be a single letter, a word, or even part of a word, depending on the language model's design. For example:

- "Apple" might count as **one token**.
- "Artificial intelligence" might count as **three tokens** — "Artificial," "intelli," and "gence."

Tokens are how AI breaks your text into manageable pieces for understanding, prediction, and response generation.
They are to language models what **bits and bytes** are to computers — the fundamental building blocks of communication.

⚙️ Why Tokens Matter in Prompt Engineering

Every prompt you send to an AI is converted into tokens before the model begins to "think." When you type a sentence, the system doesn't see words; it sees **token sequences** arranged in specific patterns.
Each token has meaning, probability, and position within a context window — and this determines how the model interprets your intent.

- **Clarity of your prompt** depends on token selection.
- **Cost and efficiency** of AI use depend on token count (most platforms charge per token).
- **Accuracy of responses** depends on how tokens connect logically in context.

Prompt engineers who understand tokens can control how much information to include, how to shape the tone, and how to avoid "token overflow" errors that cut off responses.

🧠 Key Insight for Readers

Think of tokens as **the vocabulary of AI thought**.
Every idea you express to a language model is translated into tokens, and every idea the AI returns is built from them.
Learning to "think in tokens" helps you write sharper prompts, manage limits, and predict how an AI will respond.

🔡 The Token Family Tree

Member	Definition	Typical Size / Meaning	Used For
Token	The smallest unit of meaning recognized by an AI model	Can be a single character, word, or part of a word	Understanding and generating text
Sub-Token	A fragment of a larger word	For example, "computa" + "tion" = "computation"	Language segmentation in AI
Context Window	The total number of tokens an AI model can "remember" at once	GPT-4: ~128K tokens; Gemini 2.0: up to 1M tokens	Maintaining conversation history and coherence
Input Tokens	Tokens you send to the model	Each character, space, or punctuation mark contributes	Determines cost and complexity of a prompt
Output Tokens	Tokens generated by the model	The response size in text form	Affects completeness and quality of answers
Token Limit	The model's maximum token capacity	Once exceeded, the earliest tokens are forgotten	Memory management in long conversations
Tokenization	The process of breaking text into tokens	Example: "I love AI." → ["I", "love", "AI", "."]	Model's preprocessing step
Embeddings	Numeric representation of tokens in multidimensional space	Used to measure similarity between ideas or words	Semantic search and AI reasoning
Token Probability	Likelihood of each token following the last one	Governs how the model predicts the next word	Core to AI text generation
Compression Token	Tokens that summarize or condense long input	Used in memory-efficient models	Long context compression and summarization

🌍 Analogy for Everyday Readers

If language is a song, **tokens are the notes**.
AI doesn't hear your sentences all at once — it plays them note by note, predicting what should come next based on the tune you're creating with your prompt.

💬 Quick Takeaway

Tokens are the heartbeat of every conversation with AI.
The better you understand how they flow, the more fluent you become in speaking the language of machines.

🧩 *The Parameter Family*

Definition and Overview

The **Parameter Family** represents the *memory and intelligence* of artificial intelligence models.
Parameters are the adjustable values — or "weights" — inside a neural network that determine how an AI processes information, makes predictions, and learns patterns.

Each parameter acts like a **tiny decision-maker**.
When combined, millions or billions of parameters form complex systems capable of language understanding, image recognition, and reasoning.
For example:

- A small model might have **100 million parameters**.
- A large model like GPT-4 or Gemini may have **over a trillion parameters**.

In simple terms:

Tokens are the words AI reads.
Parameters are how AI remembers what those words mean.

Why Parameters Matter in AI and Prompt Engineering

Parameters determine the *quality, accuracy, and style* of an AI's response.
They are what make one model creative and another factual, one brief and another verbose.
When you send a prompt, your text activates specific networks of parameters that were adjusted during training — this is how the model "knows" how to reply.

Key impacts of parameters:

- **Precision:** More parameters can improve nuance, logic, and accuracy.
- **Creativity:** Well-tuned parameters allow models to generate new, coherent ideas.
- **Control:** Fine-tuned models (custom-trained) adjust parameters for specific industries, tones, or audiences.

Prompt engineers often "work around" parameters — not by changing them directly, but by learning to *influence* them through better instructions, role cues, and structure.

🧠 Key Insight for Readers

Think of parameters as the **neurons of artificial intelligence**.
Each one contributes a tiny piece of knowledge.
Together, they shape the model's personality, expertise, and logic.

Every time you prompt an AI effectively, you are *activating the right cluster of parameters* to produce a meaningful answer.

🧮 *The Parameter Family Tree*

Member	Definition	Scale / Size	Used For
Parameter	A numeric value (weight) adjusted during training	Ranges from thousands to trillions	Defines how input data is interpreted
Weight	The strength of a connection between two neurons	Controls how signals travel through layers	Model learning and prediction
Bias	A constant value added to help the model adjust	Prevents uniform outputs	Balancing outputs for realism
Layer	A collection of parameters working together	Input, hidden, and output layers	Processing information at different stages
Node / Neuron	A computational unit holding parameter values	The "cells" of a neural network	Information transfer and activation
Activation Function	Formula that decides if a neuron activates	e.g., ReLU, Sigmoid, Softmax	Adds non-linear decision power
Gradient	Rate of change in parameters during training	Guides updates through backpropagation	Learning efficiency
Training Epoch	A full cycle through the dataset	Adjusts parameters incrementally	Model learning iteration
Fine-Tuned Parameter	Adjusted after initial training	Specialization for niche tasks	Industry or domain customization
Frozen Parameter	Locked value not updated during training	Reduces overfitting, speeds up learning	Transfer learning models

🌍 Analogy for Everyday Readers

If tokens are the *words* of AI, parameters are the *understanding behind those words*.
Each parameter is like a muscle fiber — on its own, small and simple, but when billions move in harmony, they create intelligence.

⚡ How Parameters Connect to Energy (Watts Family)

Every parameter consumes energy to store, update, and compute.
The more parameters a model has, the greater its **energy footprint** during training and inference.
This is why researchers focus on **parameter-efficient tuning (PET)** — making AI smarter without increasing energy use.

💬 Quick Takeaway

Parameters are the memories and instincts of AI.
They hold what the model has learned, guiding every response, every decision, and every word that follows.

🧠 The Neural Network Family

Definition and Overview

The **Neural Network Family** forms the structural foundation of modern artificial intelligence.
Inspired by the human brain, a neural network is made up of layers of interconnected nodes (or "neurons") that process information, recognize patterns, and make predictions.

Each neuron in a network receives input, performs a simple calculation, and passes the result to the next layer. When millions or billions of these neurons work together, they can learn to identify faces, understand language, compose music, or even carry on a conversation.

In short:

Neural networks are **how AI thinks.**
Parameters are **what AI remembers.**
Tokens are **what AI reads and writes.**

This family powers everything from chatbots and recommendation engines to self-driving cars and medical image analysis.

⚙️ Why Neural Networks Matter in AI and Prompt Engineering

When you type a prompt, your words are converted into tokens and sent through the model's **neural architecture**.
Each layer of this network interprets the text at a different level:

- Some layers detect grammar and word order.
- Others extract meaning and emotional tone.
- The deepest layers connect everything to context and reasoning.

The **structure** of a neural network determines how intelligently and efficiently a model responds to prompts.
A prompt engineer who understands this process can design instructions that align better with how neural networks process language — resulting in clearer, more logical, and more creative outputs.

🧩 Key Insight for Readers

Neural networks don't "think" like humans — but they *learn* through exposure and repetition. Just as people improve through practice, networks improve through **training**, gradually adjusting their internal parameters until they can predict accurate outcomes.

When you communicate with AI, you're not just talking to a machine; you're interacting with a digital brain built on mathematical neurons and connections.

🧬 *The Neural Network Family Tree*

Member	Definition	Purpose	Example / Application
Neuron (Node)	Basic unit of computation that processes input data	Performs calculations and passes results forward	Like brain cells for AI
Layer	A group of neurons working together	Extracts patterns or features from input	Input, hidden, and output layers
Feedforward Network	Data moves in one direction only	Simplest type of neural network	Basic prediction tasks
Recurrent Neural Network (RNN)	Loops information through time	Handles sequences like text and speech	Language modeling, time-series analysis
Convolutional Neural Network (CNN)	Uses filters to process spatial data	Detects edges, shapes, and patterns	Image recognition, computer vision

Member	Definition	Purpose	Example / Application
Transformer Network	Uses self-attention to process all tokens at once	Foundation of modern LLMs	GPT, Gemini, Claude, Mistral
Activation Function	Determines if a neuron "fires" or stays inactive	Adds non-linearity for complex decision-making	ReLU, Sigmoid, Softmax
Loss Function	Measures error between prediction and truth	Guides model training	Mean Squared Error, Cross Entropy
Backpropagation	Algorithm that adjusts parameters to reduce error	Core of machine learning	Used in every deep learning model
Attention Mechanism	Focuses on important parts of the input sequence	Improves context understanding	Critical in transformers and chatbots

🌍 Analogy for Everyday Readers

If an AI model were a human brain:

- **Neurons** are individual brain cells.
- **Layers** are brain regions that specialize in different tasks.
- **Connections (parameters)** are synapses that strengthen with learning.

When you prompt AI, your words travel through this digital brain — activating pathways that have learned how to reason, write, and respond.

⚡ The Role of Energy (Watts Family)

Every neural network operation — from one neuron firing to a million-layer transformer running — consumes energy.
Training a deep network can require **megawatts of power**, while efficient inference depends on chip design and model optimization.
Balancing performance with energy efficiency is a major engineering challenge in modern AI.

💬 Quick Takeaway

The Neural Network Family is the mind of AI.
It connects memory (parameters), language (tokens), and power (watts) into one intelligent system capable of learning from data and responding to you in real time.

💡 *What Is a "Chip Family"?*

In computing and electronics, a **chip** (or microchip / integrated circuit) is a small electronic device made from semiconductor material that contains many transistors, resistors, and other components. A **chip family** refers to a series of related chips sharing core architecture, design principles, or functional roles. For example, a chip family might include variants for higher performance, more memory, lower power use, or specialized features.

Chip families are important because:

- They simplify design reuse. Engineers can build for one architecture and scale up/down.
- They offer predictable upgrades. You can move within a family without redesigning entirely.
- They allow specialization (e.g. general CPU, graphics, AI accelerator, DSP) under a common interface.

In the world of prompt engineering and AI, knowing about chips matters because AI models run on **accelerators** (GPUs, TPUs, NPUs), which are specialized chips optimized for parallel computation — matrix math, tensor operations, etc. The choice of chip family affects model speed, power, cost, and capabilities.

🗂 *The Dataset Family*

Definition and Overview

The **Dataset Family** represents the *knowledge and experience* of artificial intelligence.
A **dataset** is a structured collection of information used to train, test, and evaluate AI models. It is the digital equivalent of memory, textbooks, and life experience combined.

Datasets teach machines how to recognize patterns, translate languages, generate images, and respond intelligently to prompts.
Without data, no neural network — no matter how powerful — could ever learn.

In short:

The Dataset Family is to AI what experience is to humans — the source of all learning, reasoning, and understanding.

AI models like GPT, Gemini, and Claude learn from vast collections of text, images, code, and audio. These collections form their worldviews — shaping how they interpret your prompts and generate answers.

⚙ *Why Datasets Matter in AI and Prompt Engineering*

Every AI's response is based on the information it was trained on.
When you prompt an AI, it doesn't access the internet directly (unless connected in real time); it draws from patterns it learned during training.

That means the **quality of a model's dataset** determines the quality of its responses.

- **High-quality, diverse data** = accurate, balanced, and creative outputs.
- **Poor or biased data** = limited, repetitive, or misleading results.

For prompt engineers, understanding datasets helps explain why certain models excel at technical writing while others perform better at storytelling.
It also helps users craft prompts that align with a model's strengths — or compensate for its blind spots.

🧠 Key Insight for Readers

AI doesn't "know" facts — it recognizes *patterns of language and logic* learned from data.
Datasets are not just information; they are **imprints of human knowledge** encoded in digital form.
Every bias, truth, innovation, and error in our world is reflected in them.

When you understand how datasets shape AI's behavior, you learn how to *guide* that behavior through careful prompting.

📚 *The Dataset Family Tree*

Member	Definition	Example	Used For
Dataset	A structured collection of data used for training	Wikipedia text, image libraries, or speech recordings	Teaching AI concepts and patterns
Training Dataset	The main data the model learns from	Massive text or image archives	Learning relationships and patterns
Validation Dataset	Data used to test accuracy during training	Separate from training data	Preventing overfitting and bias
Test Dataset	Final evaluation data	New examples never seen before	Measuring model performance
Labeled Dataset	Data with predefined tags or answers	Image labeled "dog" or "cat"	Supervised learning
Unlabeled Dataset	Data without categories or answers	Raw text, photos, or videos	Unsupervised or self-learning AI
Synthetic Dataset	Artificially generated data	AI-generated images or sentences	Expanding limited datasets safely
Multimodal Dataset	Contains more than one data type	Text, images, and sound together	Training multimodal AIs like Gemini

Member	Definition	Example	Used For
Balanced Dataset	Equal representation of categories	Equal gender or region samples	Reducing bias and improving fairness
Open Dataset	Freely available for research	COCO, ImageNet, Common Crawl	Publicly accessible training data

🌑 Analogy for Everyday Readers

If a **neural network** is the brain,
and **parameters** are the neurons,
then the **Dataset Family** is the *world the AI grew up in.*

Just like people are shaped by their experiences, AI is shaped by its data.
If it learns from biased, incomplete, or repetitive sources, its "personality" and accuracy will reflect that.

⚡ *The Energy Connection (Watts Family)*

Datasets also consume massive amounts of energy during training.
Feeding billions of data samples through neural networks requires weeks or even months of continuous computation in high-powered data centers.
This is why sustainable computing — optimizing energy per dataset processed — is now a critical field of AI research.

💬 Quick Takeaway

The Dataset Family is the memory of humanity, digitized for machines.
Its quality defines how well AI understands us — and how accurately it speaks back.

🤖 *The AI Agent Family*

Definition and Overview

The **AI Agent Family** represents the *action-oriented generation* of artificial intelligence — systems designed not just to think, but to **act**.
An **AI agent** is a program capable of perceiving its environment, processing information, making decisions, and performing tasks autonomously or semi-autonomously.

In simple terms:

While a traditional AI model responds to a question, an AI agent **takes initiative** to achieve a goal.

These agents combine multiple "families" of AI:

- **Datasets** give them knowledge.

- **Neural networks** give them reasoning.
- **Tokens and parameters** give them language.
- **Energy and chips** give them power.
  Together, they form a dynamic ecosystem of intelligence that can plan, learn, and adapt.

⚙️ *Why AI Agents Matter in Prompt Engineering*

AI agents are at the heart of *applied prompt engineering.*
Instead of writing one prompt at a time, prompt engineers now design **multi-step instructions, goal hierarchies, and chain-of-thought frameworks** that guide agents to complete full workflows.

For example:

- A **Customer Support Agent** can answer user questions, escalate issues, and summarize chat logs.
- A **Research Agent** can gather information, analyze it, and produce summaries or reports.
- A **Marketing Agent** can brainstorm ideas, write posts, and even schedule content.

Every agent begins with a **core prompt** — a set of rules and goals that define its behavior. That prompt acts like its *personality and purpose,* shaping how it responds, prioritizes, and learns.

🧠 Key Insight for Readers

AI agents represent the **bridge between human intention and machine execution.**
Where prompt engineering focuses on *communication,* agent design focuses on *collaboration.*
Agents are built to think, remember, and act — often working with other agents in teams.

This means prompt engineers are not just writers — they're **AI architects**, designing workflows that mimic human teamwork.

🧩 *The AI Agent Family Tree*

Member	Definition	Core Function	Example Use
Reactive Agent	Responds to immediate inputs	Acts without long-term memory	Chatbots, voice assistants

Member	Definition	Core Function	Example Use
Deliberative Agent	Plans actions based on reasoning	Uses internal models to make decisions	Research or planning bots
Learning Agent	Improves performance over time	Adapts behavior from feedback	Recommendation systems
Collaborative Agent	Works with humans or other agents	Shares information and tasks	Customer service teams
Autonomous Agent	Operates independently	Executes actions without constant supervision	Automated scheduling bots
Goal-Based Agent	Follows specific objectives	Tracks and measures progress	Sales forecasting or project planning
Rule-Based Agent	Acts based on predefined logic	Simple if-then decisions	Security or compliance checks
Multi-Agent System	Group of agents working together	Distributes tasks across models	AI ecosystems or workflow networks
Embodied Agent	Exists in physical or virtual form	Interacts through motion or simulation	Robots, VR companions
Cognitive Agent	Simulates human-like thinking	Uses reasoning, memory, and adaptation	AI tutors, creative writing assistants

🌍 Analogy for Everyday Readers

If AI models are **students**, then AI agents are **graduates** — ready to enter the real world and apply what they've learned.
They don't just answer; they *act*.
They can schedule your meetings, analyze data, generate content, or even collaborate with other AI systems — all starting from the power of a well-engineered prompt.

⚡ The Energy and Hardware Connection

Every AI agent runs on energy (Watts Family) and hardware (Chip Family).
The more complex the agent's reasoning and task execution, the greater its energy and computational demand.
This is why optimizing prompts — giving clear, structured instructions — not only improves accuracy but also **saves energy and processing time.**

💬 Quick Takeaway

The AI Agent Family transforms intelligence into action.
They are the doers of the AI world — autonomous collaborators who bring prompts, parameters, and data to life.

💬 *The Prompt Family*

Definition and Overview

The **Prompt Family** represents the *language of communication* between humans and artificial intelligence.
A **prompt** is any instruction, question, or input that guides an AI system toward a desired output.
In essence, it's how we *talk* to AI — and how AI learns to *talk back.*

Every AI model, from simple chatbots to massive large language models (LLMs), relies on prompts to generate meaning.
A prompt can be a few words ("Write a poem about friendship") or a detailed directive with structure, role, tone, and context.

In short:

The Prompt Family is the *voice of intelligence* — the art and science of communicating with machines in human terms.

⚙️ *Why the Prompt Family Matters*

Prompts are not just inputs — they are **blueprints** for behavior.
The way you phrase a prompt directly affects what the AI understands, how it reasons, and the quality of its response.

Every profession, from education to law to marketing, can be transformed by mastering prompt communication.
Prompt engineering gives humans the power to:

- Direct AI creativity toward specific outcomes.
- Control the tone, accuracy, and structure of responses.
- Build multi-step workflows and automated agents that act intelligently.

The better the prompt, the smarter the AI seems.

🧠 Key Insight for Readers

Every AI model is a mirror reflecting your clarity, intent, and creativity.
If the input is vague, the output will be generic.
If the input is structured, specific, and contextual, the AI will respond with precision and intelligence.

This is why prompt engineering has become the **new literacy of the AI era.**
It's not coding — it's communication.
The Prompt Family transforms words into logic, logic into action, and action into results.

🧩 *The Prompt Family Tree*

Member	Definition	Purpose	Example
Prompt	A command or instruction that directs AI output	Initiates the AI's thinking process	"Write a 3-paragraph essay on renewable energy."
System Prompt	The foundational directive that defines how an AI behaves	Sets tone, rules, and personality	"You are a helpful assistant that writes in a formal tone."
User Prompt	Input provided by the user	Requests specific output	"Summarize this article in 100 words."
Chain Prompt	Multi-step instruction linking tasks together	Breaks complex tasks into stages	"First outline, then write, then edit the paragraph."
Few-Shot Prompt	Provides examples to teach a pattern	Guides AI through imitation	"Translate: Hello=Hola, Goodbye=Adiós, Thank you=?"
Zero-Shot Prompt	No examples given — AI relies on general training	Used for flexible tasks	"Generate 5 creative slogans for a bakery."
Role Prompt	Assigns a personality or expertise to the AI	Shapes behavior and tone	"Act as a marketing expert."
Context Prompt	Adds background, goals, or purpose	Improves relevance	"Write for a middle school audience."
Constraint Prompt	Sets boundaries like tone, format, or length	Ensures precision	"Write 3 sentences, no more than 50 words each."
Recursive Prompt	Feeds outputs back into inputs for refinement	Enables self-improvement	"Revise your previous answer for more clarity."

🌍 Analogy for Everyday Readers

Think of a **prompt** as a *conversation starter* between human intention and machine intelligence.
Just like a teacher gives an assignment, a director gives a script, or a coach gives strategy — the AI follows your instruction with its own interpretation of what success means.

You are not commanding a machine; you're **collaborating with a digital thinker.**

⚡ The Prompt-to-Power Connection

Prompts may look small, but each one activates millions (sometimes billions) of computations across neural layers.
A well-written prompt can save both **energy (Watts Family)** and **processing time (Chip Family)** because it helps the model reach the right output faster — without wasted computation.
This is why clear prompting isn't just smart; it's **efficient engineering.**

The 4 C's in the Prompt Family

Your book beautifully introduces the **4 C's Framework** of effective prompting — **Clarity, Context, Constraints, and Creativity.**
Each C represents a discipline within the Prompt Family:

- **Clarity** ensures your meaning is unmistakable.
- **Context** gives direction and purpose.
- **Constraints** create focus and discipline.
- **Creativity** brings life, variety, and originality.

Together, they transform raw AI power into usable human intelligence.

Quick Takeaway

The Prompt Family is the bridge between human intelligence and artificial intelligence.
It's how we translate intention into instruction — and imagination into innovation.

The Memory Family

Definition and Overview

The **Memory Family** represents the *cognitive backbone* of artificial intelligence — the part that allows AI systems to remember context, store information, and build continuity across interactions.

In traditional computing, memory is simply storage — a place to keep data.
But in AI, memory goes beyond storage. It allows models to *retain context* from previous inputs, *reference earlier data,* and *maintain coherent conversations* over time.

In short:

The Memory Family is the reason AI can remember what you said, understand what you mean, and build upon it intelligently.

Why the Memory Family Matters

When you talk to an AI, you are not just giving it instructions — you are building a **relationship of context**.
Every prompt, response, and clarification becomes part of an evolving conversation that the AI interprets dynamically.

This memory-driven design allows for:

- **Personalization** — AI adapts to your style, goals, and preferences.
- **Continuity** — You can build long-form projects or conversations without repeating instructions.

- **Contextual Awareness** — The AI understands references like "that idea" or "the previous answer."

For prompt engineers, understanding memory means learning how to use context effectively — when to remind, reset, or refine the AI's internal state for optimal results.

🧬 *The Memory Family Tree*

Member	Definition	Function	Example Use
Short-Term Memory	Temporary context used during a single session	Holds information briefly for continuity	AI remembering the last few messages
Long-Term Memory	Persistent memory that stores facts, preferences, or history	Retains data across sessions	AI remembering your project or writing style
Working Memory	Active mental space where current thoughts are processed	Allows reasoning and context-switching	Comparing two previous ideas in real-time
Episodic Memory	Memory of past interactions or experiences	Helps AI "recall" specific conversations	"You asked me this yesterday, and here's what we found."
Semantic Memory	Stored knowledge about the world	Powers general reasoning and common sense	Knowing that Paris is the capital of France
Vector Memory	Mathematical embedding of meaning	Enables retrieval of semantically related ideas	Finding similar words or related concepts
External Memory	Linked to external tools or databases	Extends AI's recall and learning power	Notion, Google Drive, or API-connected memory
Context Window	The limited number of tokens AI can "see" at one time	Determines how much the AI can remember per session	Models like GPT-4 can handle 128k tokens
Selective Memory	Filters what is important to retain or forget	Keeps relevant details, discards noise	Prioritizing user goals over small talk
Memory Bank	Combined system for long-term learning	Central hub for multi-agent recall	Used in multi-agent and adaptive systems

🌍 Analogy for Everyday Readers

Think of AI's memory like a human conversation:

- **Short-term memory** is remembering what was just said.
- **Long-term memory** is remembering your friend's birthday.
- **Working memory** is juggling ideas mid-discussion.
- **Episodic memory** is recalling last week's lunch conversation.

AI functions the same way — except its memory is built from data structures, embeddings, and context tokens instead of neurons and synapses.

⚡ How Memory Powers Prompt Engineering

Prompt engineering depends heavily on *context retention.*
Without memory, each prompt is isolated — like talking to someone who forgets everything after every sentence.

By designing prompts that reference earlier ideas ("As mentioned before…" or "Using the previous summary…"), you leverage AI's short-term and working memory to build deeper, smarter responses.
In systems with long-term memory, you can train the AI to *grow* — remembering your projects, tone, and goals over time.

🔋 Energy and Efficiency Connection

Every time an AI retrieves or processes memory, it consumes computational power (Watts Family) and activates neural parameters (Parameter Family).
This is why managing memory efficiently — avoiding unnecessary repetition — helps optimize both **energy use and response quality.**

💬 Quick Takeaway

The Memory Family allows AI to think in context, respond intelligently, and build lasting connections with users.
Without it, AI would be brilliant — but forgetful.

🧩 The Knowledge Family

Definition and Overview

The **Knowledge Family** represents the *intellectual core* of artificial intelligence — the systems, datasets, and mechanisms that enable AI to "know," "understand," and "reason" about the world.

In humans, knowledge comes from experience and learning.
In AI, knowledge comes from **data, models, and relationships between information.**
It's how the machine connects words to meanings, patterns to predictions, and questions to coherent answers.

In simple terms:

The Knowledge Family is the *brain of AI's intelligence* — the part that transforms data into understanding and understanding into insight.

Why the Knowledge Family Matters

Knowledge is what makes AI useful, reliable, and insightful.
Without knowledge, an AI model is just a blank slate — capable of computation but empty of meaning.

AI's knowledge base defines:

- How accurately it answers factual questions.
- How well it reasons about real-world topics.
- How deeply it understands concepts, logic, and relationships.

Prompt engineers rely on knowledge awareness to craft more effective prompts — knowing *what* a model likely knows, *what* it doesn't, and *how* to guide it toward more informed responses.

🧠 *How AI Builds Knowledge*

AI does not "know" facts the way humans do.
Instead, it **represents** knowledge mathematically through *weights, embeddings, and patterns* in neural networks.

When AI is trained, it processes billions of examples, adjusting its internal connections until it can predict what comes next — whether a word, a phrase, or a solution.
Over time, these patterns form a web of meaning that acts as its internal knowledge base.

That's why AI can answer:

- "What is the capital of Japan?"
- "Why does the sun rise in the east?"
- "How do neural networks learn?"

It's not recalling facts — it's reproducing learned patterns of reasoning.

🧩 The Knowledge Family Tree

Member	Definition	Purpose	Example Use
Knowledge Base	A structured collection of facts and information	Stores factual or logical data	Wikipedia, Wikidata, or private enterprise databases
Knowledge Graph	A network of connected data points showing relationships	Helps AI understand context and meaning	Google Knowledge Graph
Embedded Knowledge	Information encoded within AI model parameters	Powers large language models	GPT and Claude's internal reasoning

Member	Definition	Purpose	Example Use
Explicit Knowledge	Clearly defined and structured data	Easy to read and retrieve	Rules, formulas, or FAQs
Tacit Knowledge	Implicit understanding learned through patterns	Hard to define but powerful for predictions	Style imitation or natural conversation
Procedural Knowledge	"Know-how" knowledge for completing tasks	Guides actions or processes	Step-by-step instructions or skill tasks
Declarative Knowledge	"Know-that" knowledge about facts or information	Used for factual Q&A or summaries	"Paris is the capital of France."
Domain Knowledge	Specialized understanding in a specific field	Provides expertise in niche areas	Medical, legal, or engineering data
Knowledge Distillation	The process of transferring knowledge from one model to another	Optimizes smaller, faster models	Compressing GPT-4 into smaller AI assistants
Retrieval-Augmented Knowledge	Dynamic knowledge pulled from external sources	Expands AI's real-time understanding	AI connected to the web or databases

🌍 Analogy for Everyday Readers

Think of **The Knowledge Family** as a vast **library inside the AI's brain.**

- **Memory** helps AI remember *where* the books are.
- **Knowledge** helps AI *understand what's inside* them.

When you talk to AI, you're not just asking for data — you're inviting it to reason, compare, and synthesize insights across everything it has ever learned.

⚡ *Knowledge and the Prompt Connection*

Prompt engineering becomes far more effective when you know how to tap into AI's knowledge base.
For example:

- Instead of asking *"What is AI?"*, ask *"Explain AI to a beginner using simple analogies."*
  That prompt engages **declarative knowledge** (facts) and **tacit knowledge** (communication style).

You're not just accessing data — you're unlocking *understanding.*

🔋 Energy and Efficiency Link

Accessing large knowledge models requires significant computation power (Watts Family) and optimized chip design (Chip Family).
Modern AIs balance energy efficiency with memory depth — retrieving only the most relevant pieces of knowledge for each prompt.

💬 Quick Takeaway

The Knowledge Family transforms AI from a data processor into a digital thinker.
It's not about memorization — it's about understanding patterns, meaning, and relationships that power intelligent behavior.

⚙️ *The Algorithm Family*

Definition and Overview

The **Algorithm Family** represents the *thinking engine* of artificial intelligence — the set of mathematical instructions that guide how AI analyzes data, learns patterns, and makes decisions.

An **algorithm** is a sequence of steps designed to solve a problem or complete a task. In AI, algorithms tell the system *how to learn*, *how to predict*, and *how to improve* with every iteration.

In simple terms:

The Algorithm Family is the *logic of intelligence* — the invisible code that transforms data into decisions and predictions into progress.

🧠 How Algorithms Power AI

Every AI system — from simple chatbots to large-scale deep learning models — relies on algorithms as its foundation.
They determine how the model:

- Processes and cleans data,
- Identifies relationships between variables,
- Learns from feedback, and
- Improves over time.

Without algorithms, even the most powerful dataset or neural network would remain static and lifeless.

In essence, **algorithms are the teachers** that train AI how to think.

⚙ *Why the Algorithm Family Matters*

Algorithms are what separate automation from intelligence.
They allow machines to **reason**, **adapt**, and **learn** — not just follow commands.
For prompt engineers, understanding algorithmic behavior helps explain *why* AI sometimes misunderstands a question, repeats patterns, or changes tone after feedback.

Every AI response you receive follows an underlying process — a pattern recognition journey from input to output.

The Algorithm Family Tree

Member	Definition	Purpose	Example Use
Rule-Based Algorithm	Follows predefined logic ("if X, then Y")	Solves predictable problems	Spam filters, decision trees
Search Algorithm	Finds optimal solutions among many options	Guides reasoning and exploration	Pathfinding, optimization
Sorting Algorithm	Organizes data efficiently	Enhances speed and retrieval	Alphabetizing or ranking results
Machine Learning Algorithm	Learns patterns from data without explicit rules	Powers adaptive behavior	Linear regression, decision trees
Deep Learning Algorithm	Learns complex representations from large datasets	Enables vision, speech, and text comprehension	Neural networks, CNNs, RNNs
Reinforcement Learning	Learns by trial and reward feedback	Builds adaptive and goal-oriented systems	Game-playing AI, robotics
Genetic Algorithm	Evolves solutions through mutation and selection	Mimics biological evolution	Design optimization
Clustering Algorithm	Groups similar data points together	Discovers hidden structures	Market segmentation, anomaly detection
Recommendation Algorithm	Predicts user preferences	Personalizes digital experiences	Netflix, YouTube, Amazon suggestions
Optimization Algorithm	Improves efficiency and accuracy of models	Finds best solutions under constraints	Gradient descent, Adam optimizer

🌍 Analogy for Everyday Readers

Imagine AI as a chef in a kitchen:

- The **Dataset Family** provides the ingredients.
- The **Knowledge Family** gives the recipes.

- The **Algorithm Family** is the *cooking process* — mixing, heating, tasting, and adjusting until the dish is perfect.

Just as cooking methods determine the quality of food, algorithms determine the quality of intelligence.

⚡ Algorithm Efficiency and Energy Use

Not all algorithms are equal.
Some are **fast but shallow**, while others are **deep but energy-intensive**.
Training large AI models requires algorithms that can handle billions of calculations per second — powered by the **Watts Family** (energy) and executed through the **Chip Family** (hardware).

The design of efficient algorithms directly affects sustainability in AI — minimizing power consumption while maximizing accuracy and speed.

🧩 Algorithms and Prompt Engineering

For prompt engineers, algorithms explain *how* the AI arrives at its answers.
When a model gives inconsistent or off-topic results, it's often due to:

- Misinterpretation of input signals (input encoding),
- Bias in training algorithms, or
- Overfitting to certain data patterns.

Knowing this helps you craft prompts that guide the AI's decision-making — not just its output.

💬 **Quick TakeawayThe Algorithm Family is the reasoning heart of AI.**
It transforms information into understanding and enables machines to think, learn, and evolve like digital problem-solvers.

🔢 *The Logic Family*

Definition and Overview

The **Logic Family** represents the *reasoning framework* of artificial intelligence — the system of rules and operations that helps AI evaluate truth, make deductions, and connect cause and effect.

In AI, logic is not emotion or instinct. It is a formal structure — a system of "if-then" reasoning that allows machines to process information consistently and rationally.

In simple terms:

The Logic Family is the *blueprint of rational thought* — it teaches AI how to reason, compare, infer, and decide.

⚙️ Why the Logic Family Matters

Logic gives AI its discipline. It's what makes an AI system trustworthy, explainable, and consistent.
While algorithms help AI *learn patterns*, logic helps it *validate those patterns.*

For prompt engineers, understanding logic is essential because every well-structured prompt contains a logical flow — a beginning, a condition, and an expected outcome.

Without logical structure, even a well-trained AI produces vague or irrelevant results.

🧠 How Logic Powers AI

AI applies logic in every decision it makes:

- It checks conditions (if X, then Y).
- It combines facts (A and B are true).
- It eliminates contradictions (A cannot be both true and false).
- It evaluates relationships (if A causes B, what happens next?).

Logic also underpins **machine learning interpretability** — helping explain why AI models make certain predictions and how they reach conclusions.

🧩 *The Logic Family Tree*

Member	Definition	Purpose	Example Use
Boolean Logic	Uses TRUE/FALSE values to represent decisions	Foundational logic system for all computing	if (x > y) return true
Propositional Logic	Analyzes statements that can be true or false	Simplifies reasoning into yes/no forms	"If it rains, then the ground is wet."
Predicate Logic	Works with variables and relationships	Enables AI to reason about objects and their properties	"All cats are mammals. Felix is a cat. Therefore, Felix is a mammal."
Fuzzy Logic	Allows partial truths (degrees of truth)	Models uncertainty and nuance	"The water is somewhat warm."
Modal Logic	Considers possibility and necessity	Used in decision-making under uncertainty	"It is possible that X will happen."
Temporal Logic	Evaluates sequences and timing of events	Useful in automation and robotics	"If button A is pressed, then light B turns on after 3 seconds."

Member	Definition	Purpose	Example Use
Non-Monotonic Logic	Adapts conclusions as new information appears	Mirrors human-like flexibility	"If birds fly, but penguins don't, update the rule."
Deductive Logic	Moves from general principles to specific conclusions	Ensures consistency and truthfulness	Law and policy automation
Inductive Logic	Draws general rules from specific examples	Supports machine learning and prediction	Data-driven trend analysis
Abductive Logic	Infers the most likely explanation	Powers AI reasoning and problem-solving	Diagnosing a likely cause of an event

🌍 Analogy for Everyday Readers

Imagine AI as a detective:

- **Algorithms** are the detective's tools.
- **Logic** is the detective's reasoning process.

Logic helps the AI connect the dots — finding clues, testing hypotheses, and ruling out impossible conclusions until only the most probable truth remains.

That's how AI transforms data into decisions.

⚡ Logic and Prompt Engineering

A powerful prompt always follows a **logical sequence**:

1. Define the role ("You are a data analyst...")
2. State the goal ("Analyze the following numbers...")
3. Provide conditions ("Focus on values above 80...")
4. Request output ("Summarize findings in bullet points.")

This structure mirrors the way logic operates inside AI — **condition, action, result.** When prompts follow logical order, the AI understands and responds with clarity and precision.

🔋 Logic, Energy, and Efficiency

Logical reasoning allows AI to *avoid unnecessary computations.*
By applying logic trees and decision rules, AI reduces energy waste (Watts Family) and

computational load (Chip Family).
It's not just smarter — it's greener and faster.

💬 Quick Takeaway

The Logic Family gives AI its reasoning power.
It ensures that intelligence is not only powerful — but also rational, explainable, and trustworthy.

The Language Family

Definition and Overview

The **Language Family** represents the *communication bridge* between humans and artificial intelligence.
It's the system that allows machines to understand, interpret, and generate human language through symbols, syntax, and meaning.

In essence:

The Language Family is the *soul of interaction* — where words become intelligence, and intelligence becomes conversation.

Language is how humans express thought — and now, it's how we teach machines to think, reason, and create.
Through the power of natural language processing (NLP), AI systems can translate, summarize, answer questions, tell stories, and even hold complex dialogues.

Every word you type, every sentence you craft — it all passes through this family before becoming an AI response.

⚙️ *Why the Language Family Matters*

The Language Family is the foundation of **prompt engineering.**
Without it, communication between humans and machines would be impossible.

AI doesn't "understand" words like we do — it *mathematically interprets them.*
Each word is converted into a **vector**, a numerical representation that captures meaning, tone, and context.
Through this process, the AI learns how words relate to each other — just as humans learn through patterns and experience.

Language is what turns your prompt — a few lines of text — into a full conversation of understanding, logic, and creativity.

🧠 How the Language Family Works

The Language Family operates across multiple layers of comprehension:

1. **Syntax (Structure):** Understanding grammar and sentence order.
2. **Semantics (Meaning):** Understanding what the words mean.
3. **Pragmatics (Context):** Understanding what you *intend* to say.
4. **Emotion and Tone:** Understanding how you want it to *feel.*

Together, these elements allow AI to interpret nuance — the difference between a question, a command, and a creative request.

🧬 The Language Family Tree

Member	Definition	Purpose	Example Use
Natural Language Processing (NLP)	Enables machines to understand human language	Core of all text-based AI	Chatbots, search engines
Natural Language Understanding (NLU)	Helps AI comprehend meaning and intent	Powers reasoning and context	Virtual assistants, summarization
Natural Language Generation (NLG)	Allows AI to produce human-like text	Creates clear, fluent communication	Content writing, storytelling
Speech Recognition	Converts spoken language into text	Bridges voice and text input	Siri, Alexa, Google Assistant
Speech Synthesis (TTS)	Converts text into spoken language	Gives AI a human-like voice	Audio narration, voicebots
Tokenization	Breaks text into smaller units (tokens)	Helps AI process language efficiently	"I love AI" → [I] [love] [AI]
Embedding Models	Represents meaning as numerical patterns	Captures relationships between words	Word2Vec, BERT embeddings
Language Models (LLMs)	Predict and generate coherent text	Powers systems like GPT, Gemini, Claude	Conversational AI and creative writing
Multilingual Models	Understands and translates multiple languages	Expands global communication	AI translators and localization tools
Sentiment Analysis	Detects emotions and tone in language	Measures human response and feeling	Brand monitoring, empathy AI

🌍 Analogy for Everyday Readers

Think of **The Language Family** as *AI's voice and ears.*
It listens through input (reading your words) and speaks through output (writing its responses).
It's the interpreter between human thought and machine intelligence — making it possible for you to say,

"Write me a business plan,"
and receive an answer that sounds natural, thoughtful, and relevant.

Just as humans grow fluent in new languages, AI grows fluent in human communication.

⚡ Language and the Power of Prompts

Prompt engineering exists *because* of the Language Family.
When you learn to speak clearly to AI — through tone, structure, and clarity — you're essentially learning the **grammar of collaboration.**

The more precise and expressive your language, the more intelligent the AI becomes in return.
That's why prompt engineers are, at their core, **linguists of the digital age.**

🔋 Energy and Intelligence Connection

Processing language requires enormous computational power — billions of parameters working together to understand human text.
That's why energy-efficient chips (Chip Family) and optimized algorithms (Algorithm Family) are essential for real-time communication between humans and AI.
Language is not just words — it's *data in motion.*

💬 Quick Takeaway

The Language Family is where humanity meets intelligence.
It's the reason AI doesn't just compute — it converses.
And when humans learn to speak its language fluently, they unlock the full power of artificial intelligence.

How AI Understands Human Language

Artificial Intelligence doesn't truly *understand* human language the way people do. Instead, it uses advanced mathematics, pattern recognition, and probability to interpret meaning from our words. When we speak or type, AI converts our sentences into a format it can process — a numerical language of its own.

The process begins with **tokenization**, where every word, punctuation mark, or symbol is broken down into smaller pieces called *tokens.* These tokens are then translated into **vectors** — lists of numbers that capture the relationships and meanings between words. Through this transformation, words like *"teacher," "student,"* and *"school"* become mathematically related within the AI's model of language.

Once the words are represented as numbers, the information passes through a **neural network**, an intricate system of layers that identify grammar, meaning, and emotional tone. Modern AI models use what is known as the **Transformer architecture**, which allows them to analyze all words in a sentence simultaneously to determine their context. This means AI can tell whether the word *"bank"* refers to a financial institution or the side of a river based on the other words in the sentence.

After understanding context, the AI begins **predicting** what comes next by calculating probabilities for each possible word or phrase. The result is a response that appears natural and thoughtful — not because the AI feels or reasons like a human, but because it has learned from patterns found in vast amounts of text.

In essence, AI turns human language into numbers, studies patterns within those numbers, and converts the results back into sentences that sound human. It doesn't "think" — it **recognizes**, **predicts**, and **responds** based on everything it has learned.

In Simple Terms

Raw text = **Your words before meaning is attached.**
Tokens = **Broken pieces of those words.**
Embeddings = **Numbers representing those pieces.**
Response = **AI's best prediction of what those words mean in context.**

Front End of AI

The **front end** is the *visible side* — the part you, the user, directly interact with.
It includes things like:

- The chat box where you type your questions
- The "Send" button you click
- Voice or microphone input if you speak
- The AI's written or spoken reply that appears on your screen

All these belong to the *front end*, just like the front of a website or an app.
It's the **human–AI communication layer.**

What Happens in the Front End

When you type something like:

"Explain what raw text means in AI."

1. **Your message** is captured as *raw text* by the front end.
2. That raw text is **sent to the AI model** (the *back end*).
3. The *back end* analyzes the text using algorithms and neural networks.
4. The *front end* then displays the AI's response back to you.

Simple Analogy

Think of it like ordering at a restaurant:

- The **front end** is the waiter who takes your order (your words).

- The **back end** is the kitchen where chefs (AI models) process and prepare the food (the response).
- Then the waiter (front end) brings it back to your table.

So yes — when you talk to AI and it receives your words as **raw text**, that interaction is happening on the **front end**, before the message travels deeper into the **back end**, where real computation and reasoning occur.

🧠 Step 1: Input — Humans Speak or Type

When you type or say something like:

"Write me a poem about love,"
the AI first receives it as **raw text** — just a sequence of words, characters, and symbols.

Example:
`["Write", "me", "a", "poem", "about", "love"]`

🔡 Step 2: Tokenization

AI breaks your sentence into **tokens** (small units of meaning).
Tokens can be whole words, parts of words, or even punctuation marks.

For example:

"Write me a poem about love."
becomes → `[Write] [me] [a] [poem] [about] [love] [.]`

This process lets the AI handle language mathematically — like numbers instead of words.

🔢 Step 3: Numerical Encoding (Vectors)

Each token is converted into a **vector** — a list of numbers representing meaning, context, and relationships between words.

Think of it like this:

- "King" might become `[0.2, 0.8, 0.5, 0.9]`
- "Queen" might become `[0.2, 0.8, 0.6, 0.8]`

These numbers capture **semantic relationships**, so the AI "knows" that *King* and *Queen* are related concepts.

🧬 Step 4: Pattern Recognition via Neural Networks

Now the magic happens.
The AI runs your tokenized, vectorized sentence through layers of a **neural network**, which looks for **patterns** it has seen during training.

Each layer:

- Detects grammar structure ("who did what to whom")
- Recognizes meaning ("poem about love" → it's a creative task)
- Predicts what's likely to come next

This is called **Deep Learning** — thousands of layers transforming patterns of numbers into meaning.

🧭 Step 5: Contextual Understanding

The AI uses a **Transformer architecture** (the "T" in ChatGPT).
It looks at **all words in your sentence at once**, not just one by one, to understand context.

For example:

- "Bank" could mean *riverbank* or *money bank.*
- The AI looks at surrounding words to decide which meaning fits:
  - "I sat by the **bank** of the river." → river
  - "I went to the **bank** to deposit money." → finance

That's called **attention mechanism** — it helps AI focus on the right meaning.

💬 Step 6: Output Generation

After processing, the AI starts to **predict** the most likely next token — word by word, or token by token.

It doesn't "know" the answer; it *calculates probabilities*:

"Write me a poem about love."
Might lead to predictions like:

- "Love" → 0.92 probability
- "is" → 0.85
- "like" → 0.77
- "the sun" → 0.65

So the AI might generate:

"Love is like the sun that warms the soul."

🔄 Step 7: Feedback & Refinement

In interactive systems (like ChatGPT or your AI Agents), the AI adjusts its response based on **your feedback** or **conversation history** — learning the style, tone, or focus you want.

🧩 Summary

Step	What Happens	AI's Role
1. Input	You type or speak words	Receives raw text
2. Tokenization	Splits into parts	Breaks text into units
3. Encoding	Turns tokens into numbers	Represents meaning in math
4. Pattern Recognition	Neural networks process data	Finds grammar and meaning
5. Context Understanding	Transformer model focuses on words	Chooses correct sense or tone
6. Output	AI predicts words	Generates human-like text
7. Feedback	You react, AI refines	Learns your intent better

💡 **In short:**
AI doesn't truly *understand* words like humans do — it *maps patterns between words, meanings, and contexts* it has learned from billions of examples.

🧩 *The Ingredients in the Back End of AI*

Just like a chef needs ingredients to prepare a meal, AI needs key elements in its back end to process, understand, and respond. These "ingredients" work together to make artificial intelligence function smoothly and intelligently.

1. Data

Data is the **main ingredient** — the foundation of everything AI knows.
AI models are trained on vast amounts of text, images, code, and more.
This includes books, websites, conversations, and open-source materials.
The more diverse and accurate the data, the smarter and more reliable the AI becomes.

📘 *Think of data as the ingredients in a recipe — without them, you can't cook anything.*

2. Algorithms

Algorithms are the **step-by-step instructions** that tell the AI how to learn, analyze, and respond.

They guide how data is processed, how predictions are made, and how the model improves over time.
Examples include **gradient descent**, **backpropagation**, and **transformer architectures**.

If data is the ingredient, algorithms are the cooking method.

3. Neural Networks

Neural networks are **the brain of the back end**.
They're layers of interconnected nodes (called neurons) that simulate how human brains process information.
Each layer refines the understanding — from recognizing letters, to words, to entire meanings.

They are like the chef's brain that decides how to mix the ingredients to make the perfect dish.

4. Machine Learning Models

These are the **trained systems** that actually perform the tasks — like ChatGPT, Gemini, Claude, or Copilot.
A model is the result of feeding data through algorithms and neural networks until it learns patterns.
Each model has a different purpose: text generation, translation, image recognition, or speech analysis.

Think of this as the final recipe created after many rounds of tasting and testing.

5. Training and Optimization

Before an AI model can be used, it goes through **training** — the process of learning from data.
Optimization fine-tunes the model's performance to make it faster, more accurate, and less biased.

Training is like practice — the chef trying many versions of the same dish until it's perfect.

6. Infrastructure (Hardware and Software)

Behind every AI system are powerful **computers, GPUs, and servers** that handle all the calculations.
Frameworks like **TensorFlow**, **PyTorch**, and **JAX** act as the tools that hold everything together.

These are the kitchen appliances and tools — ovens, mixers, and knives — that make cooking possible.

7. Databases and Storage

All the data and learned information are stored in **databases** or **cloud storage systems**. These allow the AI to retrieve patterns or examples instantly when you ask a question.

📖 *This is the pantry where all the ingredients are kept and organized.*

8. APIs and Middleware

APIs (Application Programming Interfaces) connect the back end to the front end. They are the **communication pipes** that let your words flow to the AI engine and the answers come back.

📖 *They're like the waiter delivering dishes from the kitchen to your table.*

🧠 In Summary

The back end of AI is made up of these 8 essential ingredients:
1️⃣ Data
2️⃣ Algorithms
3️⃣ Neural Networks
4️⃣ Machine Learning Models
5️⃣ Training and Optimization
6️⃣ Infrastructure
7️⃣ Databases and Storage
8️⃣ APIs and Middleware

Together, they form the unseen but powerful system that turns **raw text** into **meaningful, intelligent responses.**

🧩 *The Code Family*

Definition

The **Code Family** represents the collection of all reusable building blocks that programmers use to bring ideas to life through software. Just like words form sentences, and sentences form stories, *snippets* of code form applications, websites, and digital systems.

Each code snippet serves as a "family member" — performing a small but essential role in solving problems, automating tasks, or making programs function efficiently. When combined, these snippets form a strong and connected structure — much like a family that works together to achieve a common goal.

Core Members of the Code Family

The Syntax Parent (Rules & Grammar)

Every language has its own grammar. Syntax defines how code must be written for the computer to understand it — including punctuation, indentation, and structure. It's the "disciplinary parent" that ensures order and prevents errors.

The Logic Sibling (Ifs & Loops)

Logic controls how a program makes decisions and repeats actions. "If" statements, "for" loops, and "while" loops are like the responsible siblings who decide what happens next.

The Data Child (Variables & Values)

Variables store information — names, numbers, or settings — that can change during a program's run. They're the "children" that keep the family dynamic, carrying the important details everyone depends on.

The Snippet Cousins (Reusable Blocks)

Code snippets are short, reusable blocks — the cousins who share helpful tricks. Whether it's a login function, calculator script, or contact form, snippets can be copied, adapted, and reused across different projects.

The Function Uncles and Aunts (Helpers & Fixers)

Functions and methods perform specific tasks, like sending an email, calculating totals, or formatting data. They're the family members who specialize in one thing — and do it well.

The Security Grandparents (Protectors)

Older, wiser, and essential — these are the parts of code that ensure your programs are safe. They handle encryption, authentication, and validation to protect user information.

Extended Family Members

- **HTML & CSS** – The *design relatives* who handle how things look on a webpage.
- **JavaScript** – The *creative cousin* who makes pages move, react, and interact.
- **Python** – The *helpful sibling* known for simplicity and flexibility in solving everyday problems.
- **C++ and Java** – The *engineers* of the family, powering games, apps, and enterprise systems.
- **SQL** – The *organizer aunt*, managing the family's memory (databases).

Family Motto

"Every line of code, no matter how small, plays a part in building something greater."

The **Code Family** reminds us that every snippet you write — even a single line — contributes to a system that can learn, solve problems, or even change the world. As you explore this handbook, you'll see how these reusable snippets connect together, just like members of a well-functioning family.

🔝 *Top 10 Chips / Chip Families (2025 Edition)*

Here's a list of widely known, influential chip families (or chip types) that are relevant in AI, computing, and system design. You can use this list as a reference in your book:

#	Chip / Chip Family	Highlights / Relevance
1	**NVIDIA CUDA GPUs (e.g. A100, H100, RTX series)**	Widely used for AI model training and inference; excellent for parallel matrix math and deep learning.
2	**Google TPU (Tensor Processing Units)**	Specialized AI accelerators built for TensorFlow workloads; high performance per watt for neural networks.
3	**Apple M-series (M1, M2, M3 with Neural Engine)**	Integrated SoC combining CPU, GPU, and neural engine; good for on-device AI tasks and low-latency inference.
4	**AMD Instinct / Radeon Accelerators**	Competes in AI compute and HPC (high-performance computing) spaces; open driver ecosystem.
5	**Intel Xeon + Gaudi / Habana chips**	Server-grade CPUs paired with AI accelerators (Habana) for enterprise-scale AI workloads.
6	**Arm Compute / Arm NPUs (Neural Processing Units)**	Low-power accelerators embedded in mobile and IoT devices for edge AI inference.
7	**Tesla FSD / Tesla Dojo Chips**	Custom chips designed specifically for autonomous driving and real-time sensor processing.
8	**Graphcore IPU (Intelligence Processing Unit)**	Designed for graph and neural network workloads; efficient for sparse operations and GNNs.
9	**Xilinx / AMD FPGA (Field-Programmable Gate Arrays)**	Programmable chips that can be customized for AI kernels, inference pipelines, or hardware acceleration.
10	**Cerebras Wafer-Scale Engine (WSE)**	Massive, high-bandwidth AI chip designed for training very large models at scale.

📕 "The Snippet Handbook: Reusable Code for Beginners"

By Susie Hala

In today's digital world, even a single line of code can make something magical happen — a button that works, a chatbot that talks, or a page that comes alive.
But for beginners, learning to code can feel overwhelming, especially when every tutorial starts from scratch.

That's why **I wrote this book — to make coding easier, faster, and friendlier.**
The Snippet Handbook is designed for beginners who want to build, customize, and experiment without fear of breaking things. Instead of drowning in complex syntax, this handbook focuses on **small, reusable pieces of code called "snippets."**

These snippets act like **mini building blocks** — ready-to-copy, ready-to-use, and easy to understand. Each one is explained in plain English, showing not only *what* the code does but *why* it works.

From simple website functions to useful scripts for WordPress, HTML, CSS, and AI projects, this book turns code into something you can *see, feel, and reuse* in your own creative way.

💡 Why I'm Writing This Book

I've learned that technology doesn't have to be intimidating — it just needs to be explained the right way.
I'm writing this book because:

- **I believe everyone can learn coding** — you just need clear examples, not complicated theory.
- **I want beginners to feel empowered**, not afraid to experiment.
- **I want to save people time**, showing that you don't need to reinvent the wheel — you can reuse what already works.
- **I want to share practical code snippets** that anyone can apply in WordPress, websites, or small AI projects — step by step.

This handbook is my way of giving beginners the tools I wish I had when I started: small, powerful, and understandable code fragments that help you build confidence with every line.

Inside You'll Discover

- What snippets are and how to use them safely
- Step-by-step examples for WordPress, HTML, CSS, and JavaScript
- How to organize, test, and reuse snippets in real projects
- Time-saving tricks to customize websites without being a full developer
- AI-related snippets to connect chatbots and web features easily

In Short

The Snippet Handbook is not just about code — it's about confidence.
It's for students, beginners, entrepreneurs, and creators who want to do more online without writing thousands of lines of code.

With a single snippet at a time, you'll build real results — and realize that technology can be simple, creative, and fun.

These snippets are **short, powerful, and practical** — perfect for beginners and for your book ***The Snippet Handbook: Reusable Code for Beginners***.

Reusable Code Snippets (Starter Collection)

Below are organized by **category**, so you can build your own "Snippet Library" section later in the book.

1. Website Snippets (HTML + CSS)

Add a Clickable Email Link

```
<a href="mailto:info@youraistudybuddy.com">Email Us</a>
```

Create a Button That Opens in a New Tab

```
<a href="https://youraistudybuddy.com" target="_blank" class="btn">Visit
Our Site</a>
```

✅ Add Basic CSS Styling

```
<style>
.btn {
  background-color: #0073e6;
  color: white;
  padding: 10px 20px;
  text-decoration: none;
  border-radius: 8px;
}
.btn:hover {
  background-color: #005bb5;
}
</style>
```

✅ Display Current Year Automatically

```
<p>© <span id="year"></span> Your AI Study Buddy</p>
<script>
document.getElementById("year").innerText = new Date().getFullYear();
</script>
```

⚙️ 2. WordPress Snippets (for HFCM or Code Snippets plugin)

✅ Remove the Admin Bar for Non-Admins

```
add_action('after_setup_theme', function() {
  if (!current_user_can('administrator') && !is_admin()) {
    show_admin_bar(false);
  }
});
```

✅ Add a Custom Login Logo

```
function custom_login_logo() {
  echo '<style>.login h1 a { background-image:
url("https://youraistudybuddy.com/logo.png") !important; }</style>';
}
add_action('login_head', 'custom_login_logo');
```

✅ Redirect Users After Login

```
function custom_login_redirect($redirect_to, $request, $user) {
  if (isset($user->roles) && is_array($user->roles)) {
    if (in_array('administrator', $user->roles)) {
      return admin_url();
    } else {
      return home_url('/welcome/');
    }
  }
```

```
}
add_filter('login_redirect', 'custom_login_redirect', 10, 3);
```

💬 3. JavaScript Snippets (For Buttons, Popups, and Chatbots)

✅ Alert Message Example

```
<button onclick="alert('Welcome to Your AI Study Buddy!')">Click
Me</button>
```

✅ Hide an Element After 5 Seconds

```
<script>
setTimeout(() => {
  document.getElementById("promo").style.display = "none";
}, 5000);
</script>
```

✅ Embed a Botpress Chatbot

```
<script src="https://cdn.botpress.cloud/webchat/v1/inject.js"></script>
<script>
window.botpressWebChat.init({
  botId: "your-bot-id",
  hostUrl: "https://cdn.botpress.cloud/webchat/v1",
  showCloseButton: true,
  theme: "light"
});
</script>
```

🧠 4. AI & Learning Snippets (Prompt-Based Examples)

✅ Simple AI Prompt Template

```
Act as an AI Study Coach. Explain this concept in simple terms for a 6th
grader:
[Insert topic here]
```

✅ Structure for Creative AI Responses

```
Role: Expert Teacher
Goal: Simplify complex ideas about AI for students.
Style: Friendly and clear.
Prompt: Explain [concept] in 3 short paragraphs with one relatable example.
```

✅ Quick Prompt for Summaries

```
Summarize the following text in 3 sentences using clear, beginner-friendly
language:
[Paste text here]
```

🗂 5. Useful CSS Reusable Snippets

✅ Center Any Element on the Page

```
.center {
  display: flex;
  justify-content: center;
  align-items: center;
  height: 100vh;
}
```

✅ Add Drop Shadow to a Box

```
.box {
  box-shadow: 0 4px 6px rgba(0,0,0,0.2);
  padding: 20px;
  border-radius: 10px;
}
```

✅ Create a Simple Hover Effect

```
a:hover {
  color: #ff6600;
  transition: color 0.3s ease;
}
```

💡 How to Use These Snippets

1. Copy the code block.
2. Paste it into your **Code Snippets** or **HFCM** plugin in WordPress.
3. Label it (e.g., “Chatbot Embed Snippet”).
4. Select where it should appear (Header, Footer, or Before Body).
5. Save and test.

🌟 In Simple Words

Reusable snippets are like “shortcuts” to build your website faster.
Instead of writing hundreds of lines of code, you use small, tested pieces that do the job perfectly — safely and efficiently.

🌟 Introduction

When I first started learning about websites and coding, I was amazed — and a little overwhelmed — by how much information was out there. Every tutorial seemed to start with long explanations and complicated setups, and I found myself thinking:

"Why can't I just have small, simple examples that work right away?"

That question became the heart of this book.

The Snippet Handbook: Reusable Code for Beginners was born out of my desire to make coding *less intimidating* and *more empowering.* I wanted to create something that even someone with no programming background could open, read, copy, and start using instantly — without fear of "breaking the internet."

In this handbook, I've gathered short, clear examples of code known as **snippets** — the tiny building blocks that bring big ideas to life. Each snippet is like a ready-made ingredient you can drop into your website, WordPress project, or chatbot system to make it smarter, faster, or more interactive.

This book isn't about memorizing lines of code — it's about **understanding what each snippet does and how it can help you.** You'll learn step-by-step how to use reusable code for WordPress, HTML, CSS, and even AI-driven features, all written in plain English.

My goal is to help beginners — entrepreneurs, teachers, students, and creators — discover the joy of technology through simplicity. You don't need to become a full developer to create something powerful. You just need the right snippets, a bit of curiosity, and the confidence to experiment.

By the end of this book, you'll realize that coding doesn't have to be complicated. It's a creative process — one that anyone can learn, one snippet at a time.

✨ What You'll Gain

- Confidence to explore code without fear
- A clear understanding of how snippets work
- Time-saving templates you can reuse across projects
- The ability to modify your website safely and effectively
- A spark of creativity that shows technology is for everyone

Welcome to The Snippet Handbook.
Whether you're updating your WordPress site, embedding a chatbot, or just curious about how code works — this book is your guide to learning in small, achievable steps.Let's build something great, one snippet at a time.

— *Susie Hala*

💡 Why Programming Languages Are Important

Programming languages are the **foundation of everything digital** — from websites and mobile apps to artificial intelligence and robotics.
Just like we use English, Spanish, or Tongan to communicate with each other, programmers use **coding languages** to communicate with computers.

Each language has its own personality, strengths, and purpose — and learning a few of them can open endless possibilities in technology, education, and business.

Python

Python is often called the **friendliest programming language** because of its simplicity and readability.
It's used in almost every modern technology field — from **AI and machine learning** to **data analysis, web development, and automation.**

Why it's important:

- It helps beginners learn fast because its syntax is close to plain English.
- It's powerful for building AI tools, data models, and chatbots.
- It's supported by huge libraries that save you time (like TensorFlow, NumPy, Pandas).

In short: Python teaches you how to think logically and creatively while solving real-world problems.

Java

Java is like the **workhorse of the programming world.**
It's the backbone of many big systems — from **Android apps** to **banking software and enterprise platforms.**

Why it's important:

- It runs on almost any device ("Write once, run anywhere").
- It's trusted for high-security, high-performance applications.
- It builds strong foundations in **object-oriented programming (OOP)** — a way of organizing code that mimics real-life objects.

In short: Java gives you structure, discipline, and stability — the qualities behind every reliable system.

JavaScript

JavaScript is the **language of the web.**
Whenever you click a button, watch a slideshow, or chat online — JavaScript is working quietly behind the scenes.

Why it's important:

- It makes websites interactive and dynamic.
- It powers both **front-end** (what users see) and **back-end** (the server side) development through frameworks like React and Node.js.
- It's essential for integrating AI chatbots, APIs, and voice commands into websites.

In short: JavaScript turns static pages into living, breathing digital experiences.

⚙️ Other Languages and Their Roles

- **C++ / C#:** Used for high-performance applications, robotics, and gaming.
- **PHP:** Commonly used for WordPress websites and server-side programming.
- **SQL:** Manages data stored in databases.
- **R:** Popular in data science and statistical analysis.
- **HTML & CSS:** The design and layout languages that form every web page.

Each of these plays a different role — but together, they form a complete ecosystem that powers our digital world.

🌍 Why Learning Them Matters

- They help you understand how technology actually works.
- They train your brain to think in **logical, structured ways.**
- They give you the power to **build, automate, and innovate** — instead of just using other people's tools.
- They connect to AI systems, allowing you to **create smarter solutions** in business, education, and daily life.

💬 In Simple Words

Programming languages are how humans teach computers what to do.
They turn imagination into creation — from websites to robots, from mobile apps to AI tutors.

Top 10 Programming Languages

1. **Python**
   - **Why Include?**
     - Beginner-friendly with clear, readable syntax.
     - Versatile for web development, data science, automation, and machine learning.
     - Consistently ranks #1 or #2 in popularity (e.g., TIOBE Index 2025).
   - **Snippet Ideas**
     - File I/O (e.g., reading/writing JSON).
     - String manipulation (e.g., formatting user input).
     - API calls with requests library.
   - **Example Snippet** (Reusable function to count word frequency):

     python

     ```
     def word_frequency(text):
         words = text.lower().split()
         return {word: words.count(word) for word in set(words)}
     ```

```python
# Usage: print(word_frequency("hello world hello"))
```

2. **JavaScript**
   - **Why Include?**
     - Essential for web development, running in every browser.
     - Supports both frontend (e.g., React) and backend (e.g., Node.js).
     - High demand in industry (top 3 in Stack Overflow 2024 Survey).
   - **Snippet Ideas**
     - Form validation (e.g., checking email format).
     - Dynamic content updates (e.g., appending list items).
     - Local storage for saving data.
   - **Example Snippet** (Reusable function to fetch JSON):

     javascript

```javascript
async function fetchData(url) {
    const response = await fetch(url);
    return await response.json();
}
// Usage: fetchData('https://api.example.com/data').then(data
=> console.log(data));
```

HTML

   - **Why Include?**
     - Foundational for web development, easy to learn.
     - Pairs with CSS and JavaScript for complete web projects.
     - Ideal for reusable templates (e.g., navigation bars).
   - **Snippet Ideas**
     - Reusable form templates with validation attributes.
     - Semantic HTML structures (e.g., article cards).
     - Accessible navigation menus.
   - **Example Snippet** (Reusable footer):

     html

```html
<footer>
    <p>&copy; <span id="year"></span> My Website. All rights
reserved.</p>
    <script>document.getElementById('year').textContent = new
Date().getFullYear();</script>
</footer>
```

3. **CSS**

- **Why Include?**
    - Complements HTML for styling, critical for web design.
    - Reusable styles (e.g., flexbox, grid) are perfect for beginners.
    - Accessible with no complex setup.
- **Snippet Ideas**
    - Responsive grid layouts.
    - Button hover effects.
    - Dark/light theme toggles.
- **Example Snippet** (Reusable flexbox container):

css

```
.flex-container {
    display: flex;
    gap: 10px;
    flex-wrap: wrap;
    justify-content: center;
}
```

4. **SQL**
    - **Why Include?**
        - Essential for database management, a key skill in data-driven applications.
        - Simple, declarative syntax suits beginners.
        - Reusable queries are highly practical.
    - **Snippet Ideas**
        - CRUD operations (e.g., INSERT, SELECT).
        - Filtering with WHERE clauses.
        - Grouping and aggregations (e.g., GROUP BY).
    - **Example Snippet** (Reusable query for user summary):

    sql

    ```
    SELECT department, COUNT(*) as employee_count
    FROM employees
    GROUP BY department;
    ```

5. **Scratch**
    - **Why Include?**
        - Visual, block-based language perfect for absolute beginners.
        - Ideal for teaching programming concepts through games and animations.
        - Engaging for younger audiences or non-coders.
    - **Snippet Ideas**

        - Sprite movement with keyboard input.
        - Score tracking for games.
        - Animated storytelling templates.
    - **Note**: Describe snippets with pseudocode or screenshots, e.g., "Use a 'when space key pressed' block to trigger a 'say Hello' block for 2 seconds."
6. **Java**
    - **Why Include?**
        - Widely used in enterprise applications and Android development.
        - Structured syntax introduces object-oriented programming (OOP) concepts.
        - More approachable than C++ for beginners, though slightly more complex than Python.
    - **Snippet Ideas**
        - Reusable class for basic calculations (e.g., a calculator).
        - File reading/writing utilities.
        - Simple GUI components using Swing.
    - **Example Snippet** (Reusable class for area calculations):

      java

```java
public class Shape {
    public static double circleArea(double radius) {
        return Math.PI * radius * radius;
    }
}
// Usage: double area = Shape.circleArea(5.0);
```

7. **C#**
    - **Why Include?**
        - Popular for game development (e.g., Unity) and Windows applications.
        - Syntax is beginner-friendly for those familiar with Java or JavaScript.
        - Growing demand in game and app development (Stack Overflow 2024).
    - **Snippet Ideas**
        - Reusable functions for game logic (e.g., player movement).
        - File handling for saving game scores.
        - Basic UI elements for desktop apps.
    - **Example Snippet** (Reusable score tracker):

      csharp

```csharp
public class ScoreTracker {
    public static void SaveScore(string player, int score) {
        File.AppendAllText("scores.txt", $"{player}:
{score}\n");
```

```
    }
}
// Usage: ScoreTracker.SaveScore("Alice", 100);
```

8. **R**
   - **Why Include?**
     - Specialized for data analysis and visualization, complementing Python.
     - Simple syntax for statistical tasks, approachable for beginners in data science.
     - Reusable plotting and data processing snippets are highly valuable.
   - **Snippet Ideas**
     - Data filtering with dplyr.
     - Basic plots (e.g., bar charts, scatter plots) using ggplot2.
     - Summary statistics functions.
   - **Example Snippet** (Reusable bar plot function):

     r

```r
library(ggplot2)
plot_bar <- function(data, x_col, y_col) {
    ggplot(data, aes(x = !!sym(x_col), y = !!sym(y_col))) +
        geom_bar(stat = "identity", fill = "#4e79a7")
}
# Usage: plot_bar(my_data, "category", "value")
```

9. **TypeScript**
   - **Why Include?**
     - A superset of JavaScript, adding type safety for more robust web development.
     - Growing popularity in professional web development (e.g., Angular, React).
     - Accessible for beginners familiar with JavaScript, with reusable type definitions.
   - **Snippet Ideas**
     - Reusable interfaces for data structures (e.g., user objects).
     - Type-safe API fetch functions.
     - Component templates for frameworks like React.
   - **Example Snippet** (Reusable typed API fetch):

     typescript

```typescript
interface ApiResponse<T> {
    data: T;
    status: number;
```

```
}
async function fetchTyped<T>(url: string):
Promise<ApiResponse<T>> {
    const response = await fetch(url);
    const data = await response.json();
    return { data, status: response.status };
}
// Usage: fetchTyped<{ id: number
}>('https://api.example.com').then(res =>
console.log(res.data));
```

Rationale for Selection

- **Beginner-Friendliness**: Python, Scratch, HTML, CSS, and SQL have simple syntax or no syntax barriers (Scratch). Java, C#, R, and TypeScript are slightly more advanced but still approachable with clear snippets.
- **Popularity**: Based on TIOBE Index (Oct 2025) and Stack Overflow Developer Survey (2024), Python, JavaScript, Java, C#, and SQL are among the top 10. HTML/CSS are ubiquitous in web development, R is prominent in data science, and TypeScript is rising in web frameworks.
- **Reusability**: Each language supports modular code (e.g., Python functions, CSS classes, SQL queries) ideal for reusable snippets.
- **Diverse Domains**: Covers web development (HTML, CSS, JavaScript, TypeScript), data processing (Python, R, SQL), game development (Scratch, C#), and enterprise/mobile apps (Java).
- **Alignment with Your Book**: These languages match your focus on accessibility (like *The Coding Symbols Handbook*) and provide engaging, practical snippets for beginners.

Exclusions

- **C/C++**: Too complex for beginners due to memory management and syntax.
- **PHP**: Declining popularity and less beginner-friendly than JavaScript/TypeScript.
- **Ruby**: Niche compared to Python for scripting/web development.
- **Go**: More suited for advanced system programming, less beginner-focused.

Book Structure Tips

- **Per Language**:
    - Overview: Brief introduction to the language and its use cases.
    - Snippets: 5–8 reusable snippets with explanations, customization options, and use cases.
    - Mini-Project: Combine snippets into a small project (e.g., Python + SQL for a data app, HTML/CSS/JavaScript for a webpage).
- **Visual Aids**: Include code comments, output examples, and Scratch screenshots.

- **Beginner Tips**: Explain how to adapt snippets, handle errors, and find resources (e.g., Python's official docs, MDN for JavaScript).
- **Progression**: Start with Scratch, HTML/CSS for absolute beginners, then Python, JavaScript, SQL, and progress to Java, C#, R, TypeScript for slightly advanced learners.

Optional Chart

To visualize the popularity of these languages (based on approximate TIOBE Index shares, Oct 2025), here's a bar chart. I'm assuming you want a visual, but if you didn't intend this, feel free to ignore it.

Grok can make mistakes. Always check original sources.

Note: The popularity percentages are illustrative, based on trends from TIOBE and Stack Overflow, as exact values fluctuate. Scratch's share is lower due to its educational niche.

Final Answer

The top 10 programming languages for your book, *"The Snippet Handbook: Reusable Code for Beginners"*, are **Python**, **JavaScript**, **HTML**, **CSS**, **SQL**, **Scratch**, **Java**, **C#**, **R**, and **TypeScript**. These languages are selected for their beginner-friendliness, popularity, and suitability for reusable snippets across web development, data processing, games, and enterprise applications. Each includes practical snippet ideas (e.g., Python's word counter, JavaScript's API fetch, SQL's grouping query). Structure your book with overviews, snippets, and mini-projects, using visual aids to enhance accessibility. If you need specific snippets, chapter outlines, or further refinements, let me know!

This book is designed for beginners, just like you, who want practical, hands-on tools to start coding confidently. We'll explore 10 popular programming languages—Python, JavaScript, HTML, CSS, SQL, Scratch, Java, C#, R, and TypeScript—each chosen for its beginner-friendliness and real-world impact. Whether you're building a website, analyzing data, or creating a game, there's a language (and a snippet) for you.

Here's what you'll find in these pages:

- **Reusable Snippets**: Each language chapter offers 5–8 bite-sized code snippets, complete with explanations, use cases, and tips to customize them. From sorting data in Python to animating buttons with CSS, these snippets are your building blocks.
- **Mini-Projects**: See how snippets come together in small, achievable projects, like a webpage, a data report, or a simple game.
- **Beginner-Friendly Guidance**: No prior experience? No problem. We start with the basics, show you how to set up your tools, and guide you through debugging common hiccups.

- **Big-Picture Skills**: Learn how to combine languages (like HTML, CSS, and JavaScript for a website) and follow best practices to keep your code organized and reusable.

How to Use This Book You don't need to read cover to cover. Start with the languages that excite you most—maybe Scratch for games or Python for automation. Each chapter is self-contained, with clear examples and "Try It Yourself" challenges to practice. Copy and paste snippets to get started, then tweak them to make them your own. By the end, you'll have a toolkit of reusable code and the confidence to apply it to your own projects.

Why I Wrote This Book

As someone who's seen the joy of coding unlock new possibilities, I wanted to create a resource that makes programming approachable and fun. Inspired by my work on *The Coding Symbols Handbook*, this book distills the essence of coding into practical, reusable pieces. My goal is to help you go from "I don't know where to start" to "I built that!"—all while having fun along the way.

Let's Get Started

Turn the page to discover the world of reusable code. Whether you're coding your first webpage, querying a database, or animating a game character, these snippets will be your trusted companions. Let's build something amazing together!

Chapter 1: Unlocking Reusable Code: Your Coding Journey Begins

Welcome to the exciting world of coding! If you've ever felt curious about how websites come to life, how data powers decisions, or how games spark joy, you're about to discover the tools to make it happen. *The Snippet Handbook: Reusable Code for Beginners* is your guide to mastering small, powerful pieces of code—called snippets—that you can use over and over to create amazing things. This book is for anyone starting their coding journey, whether you're a complete beginner or someone looking to make coding easier and more fun. In this chapter, we'll explore what reusable code is, why it's a game-changer, and how this book will help you build projects with confidence.

What Is Reusable Code?

Imagine you're baking cookies. Instead of mixing flour, sugar, and butter every time from scratch, you could use a pre-made dough that's ready to shape and bake. In coding, reusable code is like that dough: a small, well-crafted piece of instructions that you can use in multiple projects without starting over. These pieces, or snippets, are chunks of code—sometimes a few lines, sometimes a whole function—that solve common tasks. For example, a snippet might display a button on a webpage, sort a list of names, or animate a game character. Once you have a snippet, you can copy it, tweak it, and use it again and again.

Reusable code is all about efficiency. It saves you time, reduces mistakes, and lets you focus on the creative parts of coding, like designing a sleek website or analyzing data to uncover insights. As a beginner, reusable snippets are your secret weapon: they let you build projects quickly without getting stuck on the details.

Why Reusable Code Matters

When you're just starting to code, the process can feel overwhelming. You might wonder, "How do I turn my ideas into reality?" or "Why does my code keep breaking?" Reusable snippets simplify the journey. Here's why they're so powerful:

First, snippets are tested and reliable. The code in this book has been designed to work right out of the box, so you can trust it to do the job. For instance, a snippet to read a file in Python or style a button with CSS has been crafted to handle common tasks smoothly.

Second, snippets are flexible. Each one comes with tips on how to customize it for your needs. Want to change the color of a webpage button? Adjust one line in a CSS snippet. Need to filter a different dataset? Tweak a SQL query. Snippets are like building blocks—you can stack them, reshape them, and combine them to create something unique.

Finally, snippets teach you how to think like a coder. By studying and using them, you'll learn core programming concepts like loops, functions, and conditions without getting bogged down in complex theory. You'll see how a few lines of code can solve real problems, from automating a task to making a game character jump.

Who This Book Is For

This book is for anyone curious about coding, no matter your background. Maybe you're a student exploring programming for the first time, a hobbyist wanting to build a personal website, or a professional looking to automate repetitive tasks. You don't need any prior coding experience—just a willingness to try. If you've never written a line of code, don't worry! We'll start with the basics and guide you every step of the way.

The snippets in this book are designed for beginners, but they're also practical for real-world projects. Whether you want to create a portfolio webpage, analyze sales data, or build a simple game, you'll find code that fits your goals. Even if you've dabbled in coding before, this book will show you how to organize and reuse code to make your projects faster and more polished.

What You'll Learn

The Snippet Handbook covers 10 popular programming languages, each chosen for its beginner-friendliness and real-world use. Here's a sneak peek at what's ahead:

- **Python**: Automate tasks, process data, and build simple apps with clear, readable code.
- **JavaScript**: Add interactivity to websites, like buttons that respond to clicks or dynamic content.

- **HTML and CSS**: Create and style webpages, from navigation menus to responsive layouts.
- **SQL**: Manage and query databases to organize and analyze information.
- **Scratch**: Build fun games and animations using drag-and-drop blocks, perfect for visual learners.
- **Java**: Write robust code for applications, from calculators to basic GUIs.
- **C#**: Create game logic or desktop apps, especially for platforms like Unity.
- **R**: Analyze data and create stunning visualizations for reports or research.
- **TypeScript**: Enhance JavaScript with type safety for more reliable web projects.

Each language chapter offers 5–8 reusable snippets, complete with explanations, use cases, and ideas for customization. You'll also find mini-projects that combine snippets, like a webpage built with HTML, CSS, and JavaScript or a data report using Python and SQL. Along the way, we'll share tips for debugging errors and organizing your code for maximum reuse.

How to Use This Book

You don't need to read this book from start to finish. Each chapter is self-contained, so you can jump to the language that excites you most. Want to make a game? Start with Scratch. Curious about web design? Dive into HTML and CSS. Each snippet is ready to copy and paste, with clear instructions on how to use it and make it your own.

Here's how to get the most out of this book:

1. **Start with What Interests You**: Pick a language or project that sparks your curiosity. Each chapter includes a quick setup guide to get you coding fast.
2. **Try the Snippets**: Copy the code, run it, and see what it does. Experiment by changing values or combining snippets to create something new.
3. **Build the Mini-Projects**: Use the projects at the end of each chapter to practice combining snippets into something bigger, like a webpage or a data dashboard.
4. **Learn from Mistakes**: Coding involves trial and error. If something doesn't work, check the debugging tips in each chapter to troubleshoot.
5. **Explore Further**: The final chapter offers resources and project ideas to keep you growing as a coder.

To make things even easier, you'll need a computer with a text editor (like VS Code or Notepad) and an internet connection for some languages (like JavaScript, which runs in your browser). We'll walk you through setting up everything in Chapter 2, so you're ready to code in no time.

Why I Wrote This Book

As someone who loves sharing the joy of coding, I've seen how beginners can transform their ideas into reality with the right tools. My previous work, like *The Coding Symbols Handbook*, focused on breaking down complex ideas into simple, approachable steps. This book takes that mission further by giving you practical, reusable code you can apply immediately. My goal is to make coding feel less like a mystery and more like a playground where you can experiment, create, and succeed.

Reusable code is the heart of efficient programming. When I started coding, I wished for a collection of reliable snippets I could use without digging through endless tutorials. This book is that collection—a toolkit designed to save you time and spark your creativity. Whether you're building your first project or dreaming up something bigger, these snippets will help you get there.

A Quick Example: The Power of a Snippet

Let's see reusable code in action with a simple example. Suppose you want to greet users on a website. Here's a JavaScript snippet that displays a personalized message:

```
function greetUser(name) {
    return `Hello, ${name}! Welcome to my site!`;
}
// Usage: alert(greetUser("Alex"));
```

This tiny piece of code can be used on any webpage to welcome users by name. Change "Alex" to any name, and it still works. You can reuse it in a blog, a portfolio, or an online store. That's the magic of reusable code—it's simple, adaptable, and ready for action.

What's Next?

In Chapter 2, we'll cover the basics of programming and how to set up your coding environment. You'll learn key concepts like variables and loops, plus how to install tools for each language. From there, you'll dive into the language chapters, where you'll find snippets for everything from styling webpages to analyzing data. By the end, you'll be combining snippets into full projects and writing your own reusable code.

Coding is a journey of discovery, and every snippet you learn is a step toward building something amazing. Let's unlock the power of reusable code together. Turn the page, and let's get started!

Chapter 2: First Steps in Coding: Tools and Concepts

Welcome to your first step into the world of coding! Before we dive into the reusable snippets that will power your projects, this chapter lays the foundation. You'll learn the core ideas behind programming—think of them as the building blocks of every snippet in this book. We'll also guide you through setting up the tools you need to start coding in 10 popular languages: Python, JavaScript, HTML, CSS, SQL, Scratch, Java, C#, R, and TypeScript. By the end of this chapter, you'll understand the basics of how code works and be ready to run snippets like a pro. No experience? No problem—let's get started!

Understanding Programming Basics

Programming is like giving instructions to a computer to solve problems, from displaying a webpage to analyzing data. Reusable snippets are small sets of these instructions, designed to be used again and again. To make sense of snippets, you need to know a few key concepts: variables, conditionals, loops, and functions. These ideas appear in almost every programming language, and they're the backbone of the snippets you'll use later.

Variables: Storing Information

A variable is like a labeled box where you store data, like a number, text, or list. You can use variables to hold information and reuse it in your code. For example, in Python, you might store a user's name:

```
name = "Alex"  # Store the name "Alex" in a variable called name
print("Hello, " + name + "!")  # Prints: Hello, Alex!
```

In JavaScript, it looks similar:

```
let name = "Alex";  // Store the name
console.log(`Hello, ${name}!`);  // Prints: Hello, Alex!
```

Variables let you save data and use it later, making snippets flexible. For example, a snippet might use a variable to customize a greeting or store a list of numbers to process.

Try It Yourself: Create a variable called age with your age (e.g., age = 25 in Python). Print a message like "I am 25 years old."

Conditionals: Making Decisions

Conditionals let your code make choices based on conditions. For instance, you might want to display a message only if a user is over 18. In Python, this uses an if statement:

```
age = 20
if age >= 18:
    print("You're an adult!")  # Prints if age is 18 or more
else:
    print("You're a minor!")
```

In Scratch, you'd use a visual "if-then-else" block to check conditions, like whether a game score is high enough to win. Conditionals are key to snippets that adapt to different situations, like validating user input or showing different webpage content.

Try It Yourself: Write a conditional in any language to check if a number is positive (e.g., if number > 0).

Loops: Repeating Tasks

Loops run a piece of code multiple times, perfect for tasks like processing a list. For example, in JavaScript, a loop can print each item in a list:

```
let fruits = ["apple", "banana", "orange"];
```

```
for (let fruit of fruits) {
    console.log(fruit);  // Prints: apple, banana, orange
}
```

In Scratch, a "repeat" block might move a character 10 times. Loops are essential for snippets that handle repetitive tasks, like reading multiple files or drawing shapes.

Try It Yourself: Create a loop to print numbers 1 to 5 (e.g., in Python: for i in range(1, 6): print(i)).

Functions: Reusable Code Blocks

Functions are mini-programs that perform a specific task, like a reusable snippet within a larger program. You define a function once and call it whenever needed. Here's a Python function to calculate a square:

```
def square(num):
    return num * num
result = square(5)  # Returns 25
print(result)
```

In TypeScript, a function might look like this:

```
function square(num: number): number {
    return num * num;
}
console.log(square(5));  // Prints: 25
```

Functions are the heart of reusable code—you'll see them in every language chapter, from sorting data to styling webpages.

Try It Yourself: Write a function that doubles a number (e.g., return num * 2).

Why These Concepts Matter

Variables, conditionals, loops, and functions are the building blocks of snippets. When you see a snippet later—like one to fetch data from a website or animate a game sprite—these concepts will be at work. Understanding them now makes it easier to use and customize the code in this book.

Setting Up Your Coding Environment

To start coding, you need the right tools. Each language in this book requires specific software or platforms, but don't worry—they're all free and easy to set up. Below, we'll walk you through the tools for Python, JavaScript, HTML, CSS, SQL, Scratch, Java, C#, R, and TypeScript, plus a text editor for writing code. Most setups take just a few minutes, and you'll be ready to run the snippets in later chapters.

Text Editor: Your Coding Workspace

A text editor is where you'll write and edit code. We recommend **Visual Studio Code (VS Code)** because it's free, beginner-friendly, and works with all 10 languages. Here's how to set it up:

1. Go to code.visualstudio.com.
2. Download and install VS Code for your operating system (Windows, macOS, Linux).
3. Open VS Code and install extensions for your languages (e.g., "Python" for Python, "Live Server" for HTML/CSS/JavaScript).
4. Create a new file (e.g., hello.py for Python) and save it in a folder like CodingProjects.

If you prefer, Notepad (Windows) or TextEdit (macOS) work for simple tasks, but VS Code's features (like syntax highlighting) make coding easier.

Python: Automation and Data

Python is a versatile language for automation, data, and apps. To set it up:

1. Visit python.org and download Python (version 3.10 or later).
2. Install Python, ensuring you check "Add Python to PATH" during setup.
3. Open a terminal (Command Prompt on Windows, Terminal on macOS/Linux) and type python --version to confirm it's installed.
4. In VS Code, create a file (e.g., test.py), write print("Hello, Python!"), and run it by clicking the "Run" button or typing python test.py in the terminal.

Tip: Install the Python extension in VS Code for auto-formatting and debugging.

JavaScript: Web Interactivity

JavaScript runs in web browsers, so no installation is needed for basic snippets:

1. Open VS Code and create a file (e.g., script.js).
2. Write a snippet like console.log("Hello, JavaScript!");.
3. Open a browser (e.g., Chrome), press F12 to open Developer Tools, go to the "Console" tab, and paste your code to run it.
4. For full projects, create an HTML file (see below) and link your JavaScript.

Tip: Use VS Code's "JavaScript" extension for better code suggestions.

HTML and CSS: Web Structure and Style

HTML and CSS also run in browsers, so setup is simple:

1. In VS Code, create index.html and write:
2. <!DOCTYPE html>

```
3. <html>
4. <head>
5.     <style>
6.         h1 { color: blue; }
7.     </style>
8. </head>
9. <body>
10.      <h1>Hello, HTML and CSS!</h1>
11.  </body>
   </html>
```

12. Save and open the file in a browser (e.g., Chrome) by double-clicking or using VS Code's "Live Server" extension.
13. Create a separate style.css file for CSS snippets and link it to HTML with <link rel="stylesheet" href="style.css">.

Tip: Install the "Live Server" extension in VS Code to preview changes instantly.

SQL: Database Management

SQL runs on database systems. For beginners, use an online tool like **DB Fiddle**:

1. Go to dbfiddle.uk and select a database (e.g., SQLite or MySQL).
2. Write a query like SELECT "Hello, SQL!" AS message;.
3. Click "Run" to see the output.
4. For local setup, install MySQL (mysql.com) or SQLite (sqlite.org), but online tools are easier for snippets.

Tip: Use VS Code's "SQLTools" extension for local database queries.

Scratch: Visual Coding

Scratch uses a drag-and-drop interface, perfect for games:

1. Visit scratch.mit.edu.
2. Click "Create" to start a project.
3. Drag blocks (e.g., "say Hello for 2 seconds") to test snippets.
4. Save projects by signing up for a free account.

Tip: Take screenshots of block setups to save your snippets.

Java: Robust Applications

Java requires the Java Development Kit (JDK):

1. Download JDK from oracle.com/java (version 17 or later).
2. Install and verify by typing java -version in a terminal.
3. In VS Code, create Hello.java:

```
4. public class Hello {
5.     public static void main(String[] args) {
```

```
6.          System.out.println("Hello, Java!");
7.      }
    }
```

8. Run with javac Hello.java then java Hello.

Tip: Install the "Java Extension Pack" in VS Code.

C#: Games and Apps

C# works well with Visual Studio or VS Code:

1. Download .NET SDK from dotnet.microsoft.com (version 6 or later).
2. Verify with dotnet --version in a terminal.
3. Create Hello.cs in VS Code:

```
4. using System;
5. class Program {
6.     static void Main() {
7.         Console.WriteLine("Hello, C#!");
8.     }
   }
```

9. Run with dotnet run.

Tip: Use the "C#" extension in VS Code.

R: Data Analysis

R is great for data and visualizations:

1. Download R from r-project.org.
2. Install RStudio from rstudio.com for a user-friendly interface.
3. In RStudio or VS Code, write print("Hello, R!") and run it.
4. Install packages like ggplot2 with install.packages("ggplot2").

Tip: Use VS Code's "R" extension for better integration.

TypeScript: Type-Safe JavaScript

TypeScript builds on JavaScript:

1. Install Node.js from nodejs.org.
2. In a terminal, install TypeScript with npm install -g typescript.
3. Create hello.ts in VS Code:

```
4. let message: string = "Hello, TypeScript!";
   console.log(message);
```

5. Compile with tsc hello.ts and run with node hello.js.

Tip: Use VS Code's built-in TypeScript support.

Choosing Your Tools

For most snippets, VS Code and a browser cover everything. Use online tools like DB Fiddle or Scratch for quick testing. Create a CodingProjects folder to organize your files (e.g., python/, web/, sql/). If you're unsure which language to start with, try Python or Scratch—they're the easiest for beginners.

Your First Reusable Snippet

Let's combine what you've learned with a reusable snippet. This Python function checks if a number is even, using variables and conditionals:

```
def is_even(number):
    if number % 2 == 0:
        return True
    else:
        return False
print(is_even(4))  # Prints: True
print(is_even(7))  # Prints: False
```

You can reuse this snippet in any project that needs to check numbers, like a game or data filter. Try it in other languages, like JavaScript:

```
function isEven(number) {
    return number % 2 === 0;
}
console.log(isEven(4));  // Prints: true
```

What's Next?

You now know the basics—variables, conditionals, loops, functions—and how to set up your tools. In the next chapters, you'll dive into language-specific snippets, starting with Python. Each chapter builds on these concepts, giving you reusable code for real projects. Don't worry if something feels tricky; practice with the "Try It Yourself" prompts, and you'll be coding confidently in no time. Let's move on to Chapter 3 and start building with Python!

Chapter 3: Python: Snippets for Automation and Data

Welcome to Python, one of the most beginner-friendly and powerful programming languages! Known for its clear, readable syntax, Python is perfect for automating tasks, processing data, and building simple apps. In this chapter, you'll discover 8 reusable Python snippets that you can copy, tweak, and use in countless projects—from organizing files to analyzing data. We'll also build a mini-project to combine these snippets and share tips for fixing common errors. Whether you're new to coding or brushing up, these snippets will help you get results fast. Let's dive in!

Why Python?

Python feels like writing instructions in plain English, making it ideal for beginners. It's used everywhere: web developers build apps with Django, data analysts crunch numbers with Pandas, and hobbyists automate repetitive tasks. Python's versatility and huge community mean you'll find endless ways to use the snippets in this chapter. If you haven't set up Python yet, revisit Chapter 2 for steps to install Python and Visual Studio Code (VS Code). Once you're ready, create a file (e.g., snippet.py) in VS Code, and let's start coding!

Snippet 1: Reading a Text File

Reading files is a common task for automation or data processing. This snippet opens a text file and returns its contents as a list of lines.

```
def read_text_file(file_path):
    try:
        with open(file_path, 'r') as file:
            return file.readlines()
    except FileNotFoundError:
        return ["Error: File not found!"]
# Usage: lines = read_text_file("notes.txt"); print(lines)
```

Why It's Useful: Use this to read notes, logs, or data files.
Customize It: Change 'r' to 'rb' for binary files (e.g., images).
Try It Yourself: Create a notes.txt file with a few lines, then run the snippet to print them.

Snippet 2: Writing to a Text File

This snippet writes a list of strings to a file, creating or overwriting it.

```
def write_text_file(file_path, lines):
    with open(file_path, 'w') as file:
        for line in lines:
            file.write(line + '\n')
# Usage: write_text_file("output.txt", ["Hello", "World"])
```

Why It's Useful: Save data, logs, or reports to a file.
Customize It: Use 'a' instead of 'w' to append instead of overwrite.
Try It Yourself: Write a list of your favorite foods to a file and check the result.

Snippet 3: Filtering a List

This snippet filters a list based on a condition, like finding numbers greater than a threshold.

```
def filter_list(items, condition):
    return [item for item in items if condition(item)]
# Usage: numbers = [1, 5, 3, 8]; result = filter_list(numbers, lambda x: x
> 4); print(result)  # Prints: [5, 8]
```

Why It's Useful: Filter data, like selecting high scores or active users.
Customize It: Change the condition (e.g., lambda x: x % 2 == 0 for even numbers).
Try It Yourself: Filter a list of ages to keep only those under 30.

Snippet 4: Counting Word Frequency

This snippet counts how often each word appears in a text string.

```
def word_frequency(text):
    words = text.lower().split()
    return {word: words.count(word) for word in set(words)}
# Usage: print(word_frequency("the cat and the dog"))  # Prints: {'the': 2,
'cat': 1, 'and': 1, 'dog': 1}
```

Why It's Useful: Analyze text for reports, like counting keywords in a document.
Customize It: Add text.replace(".", "") to remove punctuation before splitting.
Try It Yourself: Count words in a sentence you write.

Snippet 5: Fetching Web Data

This snippet uses the requests library to fetch JSON data from a web API.

```
import requests
def fetch_json(url):
    try:
        response = requests.get(url)
        return response.json()
    except requests.RequestException:
        return {"error": "Failed to fetch data"}
# Usage: data = fetch_json("https://api.example.com/data"); print(data)
```

Why It's Useful: Pull data from websites, like weather or stock prices.
Customize It: Add query parameters (e.g., requests.get(url, params={"key": "value"})).
Setup: Install requests with pip install requests.
Try It Yourself: Fetch data from a free API like https://api.open-meteo.com/v1/forecast.

Snippet 6: Sorting a List

This snippet sorts a list in ascending or descending order.

```
def sort_list(items, reverse=False):
    return sorted(items, reverse=reverse)
# Usage: print(sort_list([3, 1, 4], reverse=True))  # Prints: [4, 3, 1]
```

Why It's Useful: Organize data, like sorting names or scores.
Customize It: Use a key function (e.g., sorted(items, key=len) for strings by length).
Try It Yourself: Sort a list of names alphabetically.

Snippet 7: Converting CSV to List

This snippet reads a CSV file into a list of dictionaries.

```
import csv
def csv_to_list(file_path):
    try:
```

```
        with open(file_path, 'r') as file:
            reader = csv.DictReader(file)
            return [row for row in reader]
    except FileNotFoundError:
        return []
# Usage: data = csv_to_list("data.csv"); print(data)
```

Why It's Useful: Process spreadsheet data, like sales or survey results.
Customize It: Add delimiter=";" for non-comma-separated CSVs.
Try It Yourself: Create a data.csv with columns "name,age" and test the snippet.

Snippet 8: Simple Timer

This snippet measures how long a task takes, useful for performance testing.

```
import time
def timer(task_function):
    start = time.time()
    task_function()
    end = time.time()
    return end - start
# Usage: def my_task(): print("Working..."); print(timer(my_task))   #
Prints time in seconds
```

Why It's Useful: Track how long scripts take, like data processing.
Customize It: Add print(f"Task took {end - start:.2f} seconds") for formatted output.
Try It Yourself: Time a loop that prints numbers 1 to 100.

Mini-Project: Personal Task Logger

Let's combine snippets to build a task logger that saves tasks to a CSV file and summarizes them. Create a file called task_logger.py:

```
import csv
import time

def write_text_file(file_path, lines):
    with open(file_path, 'a') as file:
        for line in lines:
            file.write(line + '\n')

def csv_to_list(file_path):
    try:
        with open(file_path, 'r') as file:
            reader = csv.DictReader(file)
            return [row for row in reader]
    except FileNotFoundError:
        return []

def log_task(task, duration):
    with open("tasks.csv", 'a', newline='') as file:
        writer = csv.writer(file)
        if file.tell() == 0:
            writer.writerow(["Task", "Duration"])
```

```
        writer.writerow([task, duration])

def summarize_tasks():
    tasks = csv_to_list("tasks.csv")
    total_time = sum(float(task["Duration"]) for task in tasks)
    print(f"Total tasks: {len(tasks)}, Total time: {total_time:.2f}
seconds")

# Example usage
def example_task():
    start = time.time()
    print("Doing some work...")
    time.sleep(2)  # Simulate work
    duration = time.time() - start
    log_task("Sample Task", duration)

example_task()
summarize_tasks()
```

How It Works:

- Uses Snippet 2 (modified to append) and Snippet 7 to log tasks to tasks.csv.
- Adds a log_task function to save tasks with durations.
- Includes a summarize_tasks function to count tasks and total time.
- Run it, and it creates tasks.csv with columns “Task,Duration” and prints a summary.

Try It Yourself: Add a new task (e.g., “Write code”) with a custom duration and run the summary.

Debugging Tips

Python errors can be tricky, but here are common issues and fixes:

- **IndentationError**: Ensure code inside functions or loops is indented (use 4 spaces or 1 tab). Example:
- `def my_func():`
- ```
      print("This is indented")  # Correct
  print("This is not")  # Wrong, causes error
  ```

- **FileNotFoundError**: Check the file path in snippets like read_text_file. Use absolute paths (e.g., C:/CodingProjects/notes.txt) if needed.
- **ModuleNotFoundError**: Install missing libraries (e.g., pip install requests for Snippet 5).
- **TypeError**: Ensure correct data types (e.g., int("5") for numbers, not "5" in math operations).

Tip: Use print() to check variable values during debugging. For example, add print(data) in fetch_json to see API output.

What’s Next?
  ```

You now have 8 reusable Python snippets for automation and data tasks, plus a mini-project to practice them. Try tweaking the snippets (e.g., change the CSV delimiter or add punctuation removal to word_frequency). In Chapter 4, we'll explore JavaScript snippets for interactive websites, building on the concepts from Chapter 2. Keep your CodingProjects folder handy, and let's keep coding!

Chapter 4: JavaScript: Snippets for Interactive Websites

Welcome to JavaScript, the language that brings websites to life! From buttons that respond to clicks to dynamic content that updates instantly, JavaScript powers the interactive parts of the web. In this chapter, you'll learn 8 reusable JavaScript snippets that make websites engaging and user-friendly. We'll also build a mini-project to combine these snippets and share tips for fixing common errors. Whether you're new to coding or ready to add interactivity to your projects, these snippets will help you create websites that shine. Let's get started!

Why JavaScript?

JavaScript is the go-to language for adding interactivity to webpages. It runs in every web browser, so you don't need special software—just a browser and a text editor like Visual Studio Code (VS Code). JavaScript lets you change webpage content, respond to user actions, and fetch data from the internet. Its flexibility makes it perfect for beginners, and its popularity (one of the top languages in 2025) means these snippets will be useful in countless projects. If you haven't set up VS Code or tried JavaScript in your browser's console, check Chapter 2 for a quick guide. Ready? Create a file called script.js in your CodingProjects folder, and let's dive in!

Snippet 1: Changing Text on a Webpage

This snippet updates the text of an HTML element, like a heading or paragraph.

```
function updateText(elementId, newText) {
    document.getElementById(elementId).textContent = newText;
}
// Usage: updateText("myHeading", "Welcome to my site!");
```

Why It's Useful: Change webpage content dynamically, like greetings or status messages.
Customize It: Use innerHTML instead of textContent to add HTML tags (e.g., <b>Bold text</b>).
Setup: Add <h1 id="myHeading">Hello</h1> to an HTML file and link this script.
Try It Yourself: Update a paragraph's text to your name.

Snippet 2: Toggling a Button's State

This snippet toggles a button's text between two states (e.g., "ON" and "OFF").

```
function toggleButton(buttonId) {
    const button = document.getElementById(buttonId);
    button.textContent = button.textContent === "ON" ? "OFF" : "ON";
}
// Usage: toggleButton("myButton");
```

Why It's Useful: Create interactive buttons for features like light/dark mode.
Customize It: Add button.classList.toggle("active") to change styles (e.g., background color).
Setup: Use <button id="myButton">ON</button> in HTML.
Try It Yourself: Toggle between "Start" and "Stop".

Snippet 3: Adding an Event Listener

This snippet adds a click event to any element, running a custom function.

```
function addClickListener(elementId, callback) {
    document.getElementById(elementId).addEventListener("click", callback);
}
// Usage: addClickListener("myButton", () => alert("Clicked!"));
```

Why It's Useful: Respond to user actions, like clicks on buttons or links.
Customize It: Change "click" to "mouseover" for hover effects.
Try It Yourself: Add a click listener to show a message when a div is clicked.

Snippet 4: Validating a Form Input

This snippet checks if a text input is empty before submitting.

```
function validateInput(inputId, errorId) {
    const input = document.getElementById(inputId).value;
    const error = document.getElementById(errorId);
    if (!input.trim()) {
        error.textContent = "Input cannot be empty!";
        return false;
    }
    error.textContent = "";
    return true;
}
// Usage: validateInput("nameInput", "nameError");
```

Why It's Useful: Ensure users enter valid data in forms.
Customize It: Add checks for email format (e.g., input.includes("@")).
Setup: Use <input id="nameInput"><span id="nameError"></span> in HTML.
Try It Yourself: Validate a form field for a minimum length (e.g., 3 characters).

Snippet 5: Fetching JSON Data

This snippet fetches JSON data from an API using the Fetch API.

```
async function fetchJson(url) {
```

```
    try {
        const response = await fetch(url);
        return await response.json();
    } catch (error) {
        return { error: "Failed to fetch data" };
    }
}
// Usage: fetchJson("https://api.example.com/data").then(data =>
console.log(data));
```

Why It's Useful: Pull live data, like weather or product info, into your site.
Customize It: Add query parameters (e.g., fetch(url + "?id=1")).
Try It Yourself: Fetch data from a free API like https://jsonplaceholder.typicode.com/posts.

Snippet 6: Adding List Items Dynamically

This snippet adds items to an HTML list programmatically.

```
function addListItem(listId, itemText) {
    const list = document.getElementById(listId);
    const li = document.createElement("li");
    li.textContent = itemText;
    list.appendChild(li);
}
// Usage: addListItem("myList", "New Item");
```

Why It's Useful: Build dynamic lists, like to-do items or search results.
Customize It: Add a class to the li with li.classList.add("item").
Setup: Use <ul id="myList"></ul> in HTML.
Try It Yourself: Add 3 items to a list (e.g., "Apple", "Banana", "Orange").

Snippet 7: Saving to Local Storage

This snippet saves data to the browser's local storage for persistence.

```
function saveToStorage(key, value) {
    localStorage.setItem(key, JSON.stringify(value));
}
// Usage: saveToStorage("username", "Alex");
```

Why It's Useful: Store user preferences, like themes or form data, between sessions.
Customize It: Add a getter with JSON.parse(localStorage.getItem(key)).
Try It Yourself: Save a favorite color and retrieve it with localStorage.getItem.

Snippet 8: Simple Animation

This snippet fades an element in or out by adjusting opacity.

```
function fadeElement(elementId, fadeIn = true) {
    const element = document.getElementById(elementId);
```

```
    let opacity = fadeIn ? 0 : 1;
    const step = fadeIn ? 0.1 : -0.1;
    const interval = setInterval(() => {
        opacity += step;
        element.style.opacity = opacity;
        if (opacity <= 0 || opacity >= 1) clearInterval(interval);
    }, 50);
}
// Usage: fadeElement("myDiv", true);
```

Why It's Useful: Add smooth visual effects to elements, like images or text.
Customize It: Change 50 (milliseconds) to adjust speed.
Setup: Use <div id="myDiv" style="opacity: 0">Content</div>.
Try It Yourself: Fade in a paragraph when a button is clicked.

Mini-Project: Interactive To-Do List

Let's combine snippets to build a to-do list webpage. Create todo.html and todo.js:

```
<!DOCTYPE html>
<html>
<head>
    <title>To-Do List</title>
    <style>
        .error { color: red; }
        #todoList { list-style: none; padding: 0; }
        li { padding: 5px; }
    </style>
</head>
<body>
    <h1>My To-Do List</h1>
    <input id="taskInput" placeholder="Add a task">
    <span id="taskError" class="error"></span>
    <button id="addButton">Add Task</button>
    <ul id="todoList"></ul>
    <script src="todo.js"></script>
</body>
</html>
// todo.js
function validateInput(inputId, errorId) {
    const input = document.getElementById(inputId).value;
    const error = document.getElementById(errorId);
    if (!input.trim()) {
        error.textContent = "Task cannot be empty!";
        return false;
    }
    error.textContent = "";
    return true;
}

function addListItem(listId, itemText) {
    const list = document.getElementById(listId);
    const li = document.createElement("li");
    li.textContent = itemText;
    list.appendChild(li);
}
```

```
function saveToStorage(key, value) {
    localStorage.setItem(key, JSON.stringify(value));
}

function addClickListener(elementId, callback) {
    document.getElementById(elementId).addEventListener("click", callback);
}

// Initialize to-do list
let tasks = JSON.parse(localStorage.getItem("tasks")) || [];
tasks.forEach(task => addListItem("todoList", task));

addClickListener("addButton", () => {
    if (validateInput("taskInput", "taskError")) {
        const task = document.getElementById("taskInput").value;
        addListItem("todoList", task);
        tasks.push(task);
        saveToStorage("tasks", tasks);
        document.getElementById("taskInput").value = "";
    }
});
```

How It Works:

- Uses Snippets 3, 4, 6, and 7 to validate input, add tasks to a list, and save them to local storage.
- Loads saved tasks on page load.
- Run by opening todo.html in a browser (use VS Code's Live Server for live updates).

Try It Yourself: Add a button to clear the list and update local storage.

Debugging Tips

JavaScript errors can trip you up, but here's how to fix common ones:

- **"Cannot read property of null"**: Ensure the elementId exists in HTML (e.g., <div id="myDiv">). Check your IDs match exactly.
- **"undefined is not a function"**: Verify function names or event types (e.g., "click" in addEventListener). Use console.log to debug.
- **CORS Errors in Fetch**: Use public APIs or add mode: "cors" to fetch(url, { mode: "cors" }).
- **Local Storage Issues**: Ensure values are strings (use JSON.stringify and JSON.parse).

Tip: Open your browser's Developer Tools (F12, Console tab) to see errors and test snippets with console.log.

What's Next?

You now have 8 reusable JavaScript snippets for interactive websites, plus a to-do list project to practice them. Experiment by customizing snippets (e.g., add styles to the to-do list or fetch real API data). In Chapter 5, we'll explore HTML snippets to structure webpages, pairing perfectly with JavaScript. Keep your CodingProjects folder ready, and let's keep building!

Chapter 5: HTML: Snippets for Building Web Structures

Welcome to HTML, the foundation of every webpage! HTML (HyperText Markup Language) is like the blueprint of a house, defining the structure—headings, paragraphs, images, and more. In this chapter, you'll learn 8 reusable HTML snippets to create clean, organized webpages. We'll also build a mini-project to combine these snippets and share tips for fixing common errors. Whether you're dreaming of a personal blog or a portfolio site, these snippets will help you get started. No prior experience? No problem—let's build some webpages!

Why HTML?

HTML is the starting point for web development, telling browsers how to display content. It's beginner-friendly because it uses simple tags (like <p> for paragraphs) and works in any browser. Paired with CSS (Chapter 6) and JavaScript (Chapter 4), HTML lets you create professional-looking sites. Its reusable templates save time, making it perfect for this book's focus on snippets. If you haven't set up Visual Studio Code (VS Code) or tried HTML, check Chapter 2 for a guide. Create a file called page.html in your CodingProjects folder, and let's dive in!

Snippet 1: Semantic Header

This snippet creates a header with a title and navigation links.

```
<header>
    <h1>My Website</h1>
    <nav>
        <ul>
            <li><a href="#home">Home</a></li>
            <li><a href="#about">About</a></li>
            <li><a href="#contact">Contact</a></li>
        </ul>
    </nav>
</header>
```

Why It's Useful: Provides a consistent header for any webpage.
Customize It: Add more <li> tags for extra links or change h1 to your site's name.
Try It Yourself: Add a "Blog" link to the navigation.

Snippet 2: Responsive Image

This snippet adds an image with responsive sizing.

```
<img src="image.jpg" alt="Description" style="max-width: 100%; height:
auto;">
```

Why It's Useful: Displays images that adjust to screen size, great for mobile-friendly sites.
Customize It: Replace image.jpg with your image path and update alt text for accessibility.
Try It Yourself: Add an image from a free site like unsplash.com.

Snippet 3: Contact Form

This snippet creates a simple form for user input.

```
<form id="contactForm">
    <label for="name">Name:</label>
    <input type="text" id="name" name="name" required>
    <label for="email">Email:</label>
    <input type="email" id="email" name="email" required>
    <button type="submit">Submit</button>
</form>
```

Why It's Useful: Collects user data, like feedback or sign-ups.
Customize It: Add <input type="tel"> for a phone field.
Try It Yourself: Add a "Message" textarea field.

Snippet 4: Article Card

This snippet creates a reusable card for blog posts or products.

```
<article class="card">
    <h2>Article Title</h2>
    <p>Summary of the article goes here.</p>
    <a href="#readmore">Read More</a>
</article>
```

Why It's Useful: Displays content in a clean, reusable format.
Customize It: Add an <img> tag for a thumbnail.
Try It Yourself: Create a card for a favorite hobby.

Snippet 5: Footer with Dynamic Year

This snippet adds a footer with an auto-updating copyright year.

```
<footer>
    <p>&copy; <span id="year"></span> My Website. All rights reserved.</p>
    <script>document.getElementById("year").textContent = new
Date().getFullYear();</script>
</footer>
```

Why It's Useful: Keeps your site's footer current without yearly updates.
Customize It: Add social media links with <a> tags.
Try It Yourself: Include a "Contact Us" link.

Snippet 6: Accessible Table

This snippet creates a table with accessibility features.

```
<table role="grid">
    <thead>
        <tr>
            <th scope="col">Name</th>
            <th scope="col">Age</th>
        </tr>
    </thead>
    <tbody>
        <tr>
            <td>Alice</td>
            <td>25</td>
        </tr>
    </tbody>
</table>
```

Why It's Useful: Displays tabular data, like scores or inventories, accessibly.
Customize It: Add more <tr> rows for extra data.
Try It Yourself: Create a table for 3 books with titles and authors.

Snippet 7: Semantic Section

This snippet organizes content into a semantic section.

```
<section id="about">
    <h2>About Us</h2>
    <p>We're passionate about sharing knowledge.</p>
</section>
```

Why It's Useful: Groups related content for better structure and SEO.
Customize It: Add a <ul> for key points about your site.
Try It Yourself: Create a section for your skills or interests.

Snippet 8: Meta Tags for SEO

This snippet adds meta tags to improve search engine visibility.

```
<head>
    <meta charset="UTF-8">
    <meta name="viewport" content="width=device-width, initial-scale=1.0">
    <meta name="description" content="My website description">
    <title>My Website</title>
</head>
```

Why It's Useful: Ensures proper display and searchability.
Customize It: Update description to match your site's purpose.
Try It Yourself: Add a keywords meta tag (e.g., content="blog, tech").

Mini-Project: Personal Portfolio Page

Let's combine snippets to build a simple portfolio page. Create portfolio.html:

```
<!DOCTYPE html>
```

```
<html lang="en">
<head>
    <meta charset="UTF-8">
    <meta name="viewport" content="width=device-width, initial-scale=1.0">
    <meta name="description" content="My personal portfolio">
    <title>My Portfolio</title>
    <style>
        .card { border: 1px solid #ccc; padding: 10px; margin: 10px; }
    </style>
</head>
<body>
    <header>
        <h1>My Portfolio</h1>
        <nav>
            <ul>
                <li><a href="#home">Home</a></li>
                <li><a href="#projects">Projects</a></li>
                <li><a href="#contact">Contact</a></li>
            </ul>
        </nav>
    </header>
    <section id="projects">
        <h2>My Projects</h2>
        <article class="card">
            <h3>Project 1</h3>
            <p>A cool app I built.</p>
            <a href="#details">Learn More</a>
        </article>
        <article class="card">
            <h3>Project 2</h3>
            <p>A website I designed.</p>
            <a href="#details">Learn More</a>
        </article>
    </section>
    <footer>
        <p>&copy; <span id="year"></span> My Portfolio. All rights
reserved.</p>
        <script>document.getElementById("year").textContent = new
Date().getFullYear();</script>
    </footer>
</body>
</html>
```

How It Works:

- Uses Snippets 1, 4, 5, and 8 for a header, project cards, footer, and meta tags.
- Includes basic CSS for card styling (expanded in Chapter 6).
- Run by opening portfolio.html in a browser (use VS Code's Live Server).

Try It Yourself: Add a third project card or an <img> to one card.

Debugging Tips

HTML errors are often simple but tricky:

- **Broken Layout**: Check for missing closing tags (e.g., </div>). Use VS Code's auto-close tag feature.
- **Links Don't Work**: Ensure href values match IDs (e.g., href="#about" needs <section id="about">).
- **Images Not Showing**: Verify src paths (e.g., images/photo.jpg for a subfolder). Use absolute URLs if needed.
- **Accessibility Issues**: Add alt text to images and role attributes to tables.

Tip: Use your browser's Developer Tools (F12, Elements tab) to inspect HTML and find errors.

What's Next?

You now have 8 reusable HTML snippets for structuring webpages, plus a portfolio project. Try customizing snippets (e.g., add more navigation links or table rows). In Chapter 6, we'll add CSS snippets to style these structures, making your pages look amazing. Keep your CodingProjects folder ready, and let's keep building!

Chapter 6: CSS: Snippets for Styling with Flair

CSS (Cascading Style Sheets) is the magic that makes webpages look polished and professional. While HTML builds the structure (Chapter 5), CSS adds colors, layouts, and animations to bring your pages to life. In this chapter, you'll learn 8 reusable CSS snippets to style your webpages, from responsive layouts to eye-catching effects. We'll also build a mini-project to combine these snippets and share tips for fixing common styling issues. Whether you're designing a blog, a portfolio, or a personal site, these snippets will make your pages pop. Let's add some flair to your web projects!

Why CSS?

CSS is beginner-friendly, letting you transform plain HTML into beautiful designs with simple rules. It works in any web browser, pairs perfectly with HTML and JavaScript (Chapter 4), and supports reusable styles that save time across projects. CSS is essential for modern web design, with trends like responsive layouts and animations dominating in 2025. Its flexibility makes it ideal for creating reusable snippets, aligning with this book's focus. If you haven't set up Visual Studio Code (VS Code) or tested HTML/CSS, check Chapter 2 for a quick guide. Create a file called style.css in your CodingProjects folder, link it to an HTML file with <link rel="stylesheet" href="style.css">, and let's start styling!

Snippet 1: Centered Container

This snippet centers a container with a flexible width, creating a clean layout.

```
.container {
    max-width: 800px;
    margin: 0 auto;
    padding: 20px;
}
```

Why It's Useful: Centers content (e.g., text, images) on the page, perfect for blogs or portfolios.
Customize It: Change max-width to 1200px for wider layouts or add background-color: #f9f9f9 for a background.
Setup: Apply to <div class="container">Content</div> in your HTML.
Try It Yourself: Wrap a paragraph from Chapter 5 in this container and test in a browser.

Snippet 2: Flexbox Layout

This snippet creates a flexible, responsive row of items.

```
.flex-row {
    display: flex;
    gap: 20px;
    flex-wrap: wrap;
}
```

Why It's Useful: Arranges items (e.g., cards, images) in a row that adapts to screen sizes, great for galleries.
Customize It: Add justify-content: center to center items or flex-direction: column for vertical stacking.
Setup: Use with multiple <div> elements, like <div class="flex-row"><div>Item 1</div><div>Item 2</div></div>.
Try It Yourself: Create a flex row with 3 boxes containing text.

Snippet 3: Hover Button Effect

This snippet adds a hover effect to buttons for interactivity.

```
.button {
    background-color: #007bff;
    color: white;
    padding: 10px 20px;
    border: none;
    cursor: pointer;
    transition: background-color 0.3s;
}
.button:hover {
    background-color: #0056b3;
}
```

Why It's Useful: Makes buttons engaging, ideal for forms or calls-to-action.
Customize It: Change colors (e.g., #28a745 for green) or add transform: scale(1.1) for a zoom effect.
Setup: Apply to <button class="button">Click Me</button>.
Try It Yourself: Style a button from Chapter 5's contact form.

Snippet 4: Responsive Grid

This snippet creates a grid layout that adjusts to screen size.

```
.grid {
    display: grid;
    grid-template-columns: repeat(auto-fit, minmax(200px, 1fr));
    gap: 15px;
}
```

Why It's Useful: Perfect for product listings, photo galleries, or blog posts, with automatic column adjustments.
Customize It: Adjust minmax(200px, 1fr) to minmax(300px, 1fr) for wider columns.
Setup: Use with <div class="grid"><div>Item 1</div><div>Item 2</div></div>.
Try It Yourself: Create a grid with 4 placeholder images.

Snippet 5: Dark Mode Toggle

This snippet enables a dark mode theme for your site.

```
body {
    background-color: white;
    color: black;
    transition: all 0.3s;
}
body.dark-mode {
    background-color: #333;
    color: white;
}
```

Why It's Useful: Offers users a dark theme, improving accessibility and comfort.
Customize It: Add styles for specific elements (e.g., .button.dark-mode { background: #555; }).
Setup: Toggle with JavaScript, e.g., document.body.classList.toggle("dark-mode") (see Chapter 4).
Try It Yourself: Apply to a page and test the toggle with a button.

Snippet 6: Sticky Navigation

This snippet makes a navigation bar stick to the top of the page.

```
nav {
    position: sticky;
```

```
    top: 0;
    background-color: #f8f9fa;
    padding: 10px;
    z-index: 100;
}
```

Why It's Useful: Keeps navigation accessible while scrolling, ideal for long pages.
Customize It: Add box-shadow: 0 2px 5px rgba(0,0,0,0.1) for a shadow effect.
Setup: Apply to <nav> from Chapter 5's header snippet.
Try It Yourself: Style a <nav> from your portfolio project.

Snippet 7: Card Hover Effect

This snippet adds a hover effect to cards, like blog posts or products.

```
.card {
    border: 1px solid #ddd;
    padding: 15px;
    transition: transform 0.3s;
}
.card:hover {
    transform: translateY(-5px);
}
```

Why It's Useful: Enhances cards with a subtle lift effect, making content stand out.
Customize It: Add box-shadow: 0 4px 8px rgba(0,0,0,0.2) on hover for depth.
Setup: Use with <article class="card"> from Chapter 5.
Try It Yourself: Apply to a card from the portfolio project.

Snippet 8: Centered Text Block

This snippet centers text vertically and horizontally, perfect for hero sections.

```
.text-center {
    display: flex;
    justify-content: center;
    align-items: center;
    height: 100vh;
}
```

Why It's Useful: Creates eye-catching landing page headers or call-to-action sections.
Customize It: Adjust height to 200px for smaller sections or add font-size: 2em.
Setup: Apply to <section class="text-center"><h2>Welcome</h2></section>.
Try It Yourself: Center a <h1> with your name on a page.

Mini-Project: Styled Blog Homepage

Let's combine snippets to style a blog homepage, building on HTML from Chapter 5. Create blog.html and style.css:

```
<!DOCTYPE html>
<html lang="en">
```

```
<head>
    <meta charset="UTF-8">
    <meta name="viewport" content="width=device-width, initial-scale=1.0">
    <meta name="description" content="My blog homepage">
    <title>My Blog</title>
    <link rel="stylesheet" href="style.css">
</head>
<body>
    <header>
        <h1>My Blog</h1>
        <nav>
            <ul>
                <li><a href="#home">Home</a></li>
                <li><a href="#posts">Posts</a></li>
            </ul>
        </nav>
    </header>
    <div class="container">
        <section class="text-center">
            <h2>Welcome to My Blog</h2>
        </section>
        <section id="posts" class="grid">
            <article class="card">
                <h3>Post 1</h3>
                <p>A great story about my journey.</p>
            </article>
            <article class="card">
                <h3>Post 2</h3>
                <p>Insights on coding tips.</p>
            </article>
        </section>
    </div>
    <footer>
        <p>&copy; <span id="year"></span> My Blog. All rights reserved.</p>
        <script>document.getElementById("year").textContent = new
Date().getFullYear();</script>
    </footer>
</body>
</html>
/* style.css */
.container {
    max-width: 800px;
    margin: 0 auto;
    padding: 20px;
}
.grid {
    display: grid;
    grid-template-columns: repeat(auto-fit, minmax(200px, 1fr));
    gap: 15px;
}
.card {
    border: 1px solid #ddd;
    padding: 15px;
    transition: transform 0.3s;
}
.card:hover {
    transform: translateY(-5px);
}
.text-center {
```

```
    display: flex;
    justify-content: center;
    align-items: center;
    height: 200px;
}
nav {
    position: sticky;
    top: 0;
    background-color: #f8f9fa;
    padding: 10px;
}
```

How It Works:

- Uses Snippets 1, 4, 6, and 7 to create a centered container, responsive grid, sticky navigation, and hoverable cards.
- Combines with HTML from Chapter 5 for a cohesive, styled blog page.
- Run by opening blog.html in a browser (use VS Code's Live Server for live updates).

Try It Yourself: Add a button with Snippet 3 to each card for a "Read More" link with hover effects.

Debugging Tips

CSS issues can be frustrating, but here's how to fix common problems:

- **Styles Not Applying**: Check selector names (e.g., .container vs #container). Use Developer Tools (F12, Styles tab) to inspect elements and verify styles.
- **Layout Breaks**: Ensure display: flex or grid properties are correct (e.g., gap or grid-template-columns). Test on different screen sizes using browser's responsive mode.
- **Hover Effects Not Working**: Verify transition properties match the changed property (e.g., transition: transform for transform). Check if :hover is applied to the correct element.
- **Sticky Navigation Fails**: Ensure position: sticky has a top value (e.g., top: 0) and isn't inside an overflow: hidden parent.

Tip: Add border: 1px solid red to elements temporarily to debug layout boundaries. Use Developer Tools to hover over elements and see their CSS properties.

What's Next?

You now have 8 reusable CSS snippets for styling webpages, plus a styled blog homepage to practice them. Experiment by tweaking colors, adjusting grid columns, or adding animations. In Chapter 7, we'll explore SQL snippets for managing data, which you can pair with your web projects to store and retrieve information. Keep your CodingProjects folder ready, and let's keep styling!

Chapter 7: SQL: Snippets for Managing Data

Welcome to SQL (Structured Query Language), the language for organizing and retrieving data in databases! Whether you're tracking inventory, analyzing sales, or building a web app, SQL helps you store and query data efficiently. In this chapter, you'll learn 8 reusable SQL snippets to create, query, and manage databases. We'll also build a mini-project to combine these snippets and share tips for fixing common errors. No database experience? No worries—these snippets are designed for beginners to get results fast. Let's dive into data!

Why SQL?

SQL is the standard for working with databases, used by everyone from data analysts to web developers. Its clear, English-like syntax makes it approachable, and its reusable queries align perfectly with this book's focus on snippets. SQL works with systems like SQLite, MySQL, and PostgreSQL, letting you manage data for apps or reports. In 2025, SQL remains essential for handling structured data, from small projects to massive systems. If you haven't set up a database tool, revisit Chapter 2 for a guide to using **DB Fiddle** (an online SQL editor) or installing SQLite/MySQL. Ready? Let's write some queries!

Setup Recap

For these snippets, use **DB Fiddle** (dbfiddle.uk) with SQLite or MySQL:

1. Go to dbfiddle.uk, select SQLite or MySQL, and paste snippets in the query editor.
2. Run queries and view results in the output pane.
3. Alternatively, install SQLite (sqlite.org) or MySQL (mysql.com) and use VS Code with the "SQLTools" extension. Create a sample table to test snippets:

```
CREATE TABLE users (
    id INTEGER PRIMARY KEY,
    name TEXT,
    age INTEGER,
    email TEXT
);
INSERT INTO users (name, age, email) VALUES
    ('Alice', 25, 'alice@email.com'),
    ('Bob', 30, 'bob@email.com'),
    ('Cathy', 22, 'cathy@email.com');
```

Snippet 1: Selecting All Data

This snippet retrieves all rows from a table.

```
SELECT * FROM users;
```

Why It's Useful: View all data in a table, like a user list or inventory.
Customize It: Replace users with your table name or add LIMIT 5 to show only 5 rows.
Output: Returns all columns (id, name, age, email) for all users.
Try It Yourself: Run on the users table and check the results.

Snippet 2: Filtering Rows

This snippet filters rows based on a condition.

```
SELECT name, age FROM users WHERE age > 25;
```

Why It's Useful: Find specific data, like users over a certain age or products in stock.
Customize It: Change age > 25 to email LIKE '%@email.com' to match email domains.
Output: Returns name, age for users older than 25 (e.g., Bob).
Try It Yourself: Filter users with age < 30.

Snippet 3: Sorting Results

This snippet sorts query results by a column.

```
SELECT * FROM users ORDER BY age DESC;
```

Why It's Useful: Organize data, like sorting users by age or products by price.
Customize It: Use ASC instead of DESC for ascending order or sort by name.
Output: Returns all users, sorted from oldest to youngest.
Try It Yourself: Sort users by name alphabetically.

Snippet 4: Inserting a Row

This snippet adds a new row to a table.

```
INSERT INTO users (name, age, email) VALUES ('Dave', 28, 'dave@email.com');
```

Why It's Useful: Add new data, like a new user or order.
Customize It: Adjust column names and values to match your table.
Try It Yourself: Insert a user with your name and age.

Snippet 5: Updating Rows

This snippet updates existing rows based on a condition.

```
UPDATE users SET age = age + 1 WHERE name = 'Alice';
```

Why It's Useful: Modify data, like updating ages or statuses.
Customize It: Change age = age + 1 to email = 'new@email.com' or use a different WHERE condition.
Output: Increases Alice's age by 1.
Try It Yourself: Update Bob's email to a new address.

Snippet 6: Deleting Rows

This snippet deletes rows matching a condition.

```
DELETE FROM users WHERE age < 25;
```

Why It's Useful: Remove unwanted data, like inactive users or old records.
Customize It: Use WHERE id = 1 to delete a specific row by ID.
Output: Deletes users under 25 (e.g., Cathy).
Try It Yourself: Delete users with a specific email domain.

Snippet 7: Joining Tables

This snippet joins two tables to combine data.

```
CREATE TABLE orders (
    order_id INTEGER PRIMARY KEY,
    user_id INTEGER,
    product TEXT
);
INSERT INTO orders (user_id, product) VALUES (1, 'Laptop'), (2, 'Phone');
SELECT users.name, orders.product
FROM users
JOIN orders ON users.id = orders.user_id;
```

Why It's Useful: Combine related data, like users and their orders.
Customize It: Use LEFT JOIN to include users without orders or change columns selected.
Output: Returns names and their products (e.g., Alice-Laptop, Bob-Phone).
Try It Yourself: Create an orders table and join it with users.

Snippet 8: Aggregating Data

This snippet counts rows or calculates aggregates.

```
SELECT COUNT(*) AS user_count, AVG(age) AS avg_age FROM users;
```

Why It's Useful: Summarize data, like counting users or averaging ages.
Customize It: Use SUM(age) or MAX(age) for different aggregates.
Output: Returns the number of users and their average age.
Try It Yourself: Calculate the total number of users with age > 20.

Mini-Project: User Management Dashboard

Let's combine snippets to create a simple user management system. Use DB Fiddle or a local SQLite/MySQL database. Run these queries to set up and manage a users table:

```
-- Create and populate table
CREATE TABLE users (
    id INTEGER PRIMARY KEY,
    name TEXT,
    age INTEGER,
    email TEXT
);
INSERT INTO users (name, age, email) VALUES
    ('Alice', 25, 'alice@email.com'),
    ('Bob', 30, 'bob@email.com'),
    ('Cathy', 22, 'cathy@email.com');
```

```
-- Snippet 4: Add a new user
INSERT INTO users (name, age, email) VALUES ('Eve', 27, 'eve@email.com');

-- Snippet 2: Filter users over 25
SELECT name, age, email FROM users WHERE age > 25;

-- Snippet 3: Sort by name
SELECT * FROM users ORDER BY name ASC;

-- Snippet 5: Update an email
UPDATE users SET email = 'cathy.new@email.com' WHERE name = 'Cathy';

-- Snippet 8: Summarize data
SELECT COUNT(*) AS total_users, AVG(age) AS avg_age FROM users;
```

How It Works:

- Uses Snippets 2, 3, 4, 5, and 8 to add, filter, sort, update, and summarize user data.
- Creates a users table and performs common management tasks.
- Run each query in DB Fiddle to see results (e.g., filtered users, summary stats).

Try It Yourself: Add a new user, then filter for users with age < 30 and sort by email.

Debugging Tips

SQL errors can be tricky, but here's how to fix common issues:

- **"No such table"**: Ensure the table exists (e.g., run CREATE TABLE first). Check table names for typos.
- **"Syntax error near…"**: Verify commas, semicolons, and keywords (e.g., SELECT not SELEC). Use DB Fiddle's error messages to pinpoint issues.
- **"Column not found"**: Check column names in SELECT or WHERE match the table (e.g., users.age not users.Age).
- **No Results from JOIN**: Ensure ON conditions match (e.g., users.id = orders.user_id). Use LEFT JOIN to include unmatched rows.

Tip: Use SELECT * FROM table_name LIMIT 5; to preview table data before running complex queries.

What's Next?

You now have 8 reusable SQL snippets for managing data, plus a user management dashboard to practice them. Experiment by tweaking queries (e.g., filter by email or join with a new table). In Chapter 8, we'll explore Scratch snippets for creating fun games and animations, perfect for visual learners. Keep your database tool or DB Fiddle ready, and let's keep querying!

Chapter 8: Scratch: Snippets for Visual Coding and Games

Welcome to Scratch, a fun, visual programming language where you drag and drop blocks to create games, animations, and stories! Scratch is perfect for beginners because it skips complex syntax, letting you focus on coding logic through colorful blocks. In this chapter, you'll learn 8 reusable Scratch snippets to build interactive projects, from moving sprites to tracking scores. We'll also create a mini-project—a simple game—and share tips for fixing common issues. Whether you're new to coding or want to make something fun, these snippets will spark your creativity. Let's start building in Scratch!

Why Scratch?

Scratch, developed by MIT, is designed for beginners, making it easy to create games and animations without typing code. Its drag-and-drop interface teaches core programming concepts like loops, conditionals, and variables, which apply to languages like Python (Chapter 3) or JavaScript (Chapter 4). Scratch is widely used in 2025 for education and hobby projects, and its reusable snippets fit this book's focus. You'll use Scratch's online editor (scratch.mit.edu) or offline version—no extra software needed beyond a browser or the Scratch app. If you haven't tried Scratch, check Chapter 2 for a guide to set up a Scratch account and create a new project. Ready? Open Scratch, create a new project, and let's code visually!

Setup Recap

1. Go to scratch.mit.edu, click "Create," or download the Scratch app.
2. Choose a sprite (e.g., Scratch Cat) and a backdrop (e.g., blank stage).
3. Use the "Code" tab to drag blocks from the left palette to the scripts area.
4. Test snippets by clicking the green flag or individual blocks. For snippets, we'll describe block sequences as pseudocode (e.g., "When green flag clicked, move 10 steps"). Replicate these in Scratch by dragging the corresponding blocks.

Snippet 1: Move a Sprite

This snippet moves a sprite across the stage when the green flag is clicked.

```
When green flag clicked
Forever
    Move 10 steps
    If touching edge, bounce
```

Why It's Useful: Creates basic movement for games or animations, like a character walking.
Customize It: Change 10 steps to 20 for faster movement or add Turn 15 degrees for rotation.
Setup: Select a sprite (e.g., Scratch Cat) and drag these blocks from "Events" and "Motion."
Try It Yourself: Make the sprite move diagonally by adding Change Y by 5.

Snippet 2: Change Costume

This snippet switches a sprite's costume to animate it.

```
When green flag clicked
Forever
    Switch costume to next costume
    Wait 0.5 seconds
```

Why It's Useful: Animates sprites, like a walking character or blinking eyes.
Customize It: Use Switch costume to [costume name] for specific costumes or adjust Wait 0.3 seconds for faster animation.
Setup: Choose a sprite with multiple costumes (e.g., Cat's "cat-a" and "cat-b").
Try It Yourself: Animate a sprite with 3 costumes.

Snippet 3: Respond to Key Press

This snippet moves a sprite when a key is pressed.

```
When [space] key pressed
Change X by 10
```

Why It's Useful: Adds user control, like moving a player in a game.
Customize It: Change space to right arrow or use Change Y by 10 for vertical movement.
Setup: Use "Events" and "Motion" blocks.
Try It Yourself: Make a sprite move left with the left arrow key.

Snippet 4: Play a Sound

This snippet plays a sound when a sprite is clicked.

```
When this sprite clicked
Play sound [pop] until done
```

Why It's Useful: Adds audio feedback, like a sound effect in a game.
Customize It: Choose a different sound (e.g., meow) from the "Sounds" tab or add Start sound [meow] for overlapping sounds.
Setup: Add a sound to your sprite via the "Sounds" tab.
Try It Yourself: Play a sound when the up arrow is pressed.

Snippet 5: Keep Score

This snippet tracks a score using a variable.

```
When green flag clicked
Set [score] to 0
Forever
    If touching [Sprite2]
        Change [score] by 1
        Wait 1 second
```

Why It's Useful: Tracks points in games, like collecting coins.
Customize It: Change Sprite2 to another sprite or use Change [score] by -1 for penalties.
Setup: Create a score variable in the "Variables" tab and add a second sprite.
Try It Yourself: Increase the score when the sprite touches a specific backdrop area.

Snippet 6: Show/Hide Sprite

This snippet shows or hides a sprite based on a condition.

```
When green flag clicked
Forever
    If [mouse down?]
        Show
    Else
        Hide
```

Why It's Useful: Creates interactive effects, like revealing a sprite on click.
Customize It: Replace mouse down? with touching [Sprite2]? or use When [c] key pressed to toggle visibility.
Try It Yourself: Hide a sprite when it touches another sprite.

Snippet 7: Broadcast Message

This snippet sends a message to trigger actions across sprites.

```
When green flag clicked
When I receive [startGame]
Move 50 steps
Broadcast [endGame]
```

Why It's Useful: Coordinates actions, like starting a game or changing scenes.
Customize It: Create a new message (e.g., levelUp) or add actions like Switch backdrop to [next backdrop].
Setup: Use "Events" blocks and create messages in the "Broadcast" dropdown.
Try It Yourself: Broadcast a message to make another sprite jump.

Snippet 8: Random Movement

This snippet makes a sprite move to a random position.

```
When green flag clicked
Forever
    Go to x: [random -240 to 240] y: [random -180 to 180]
    Wait 1 second
```

Why It's Useful: Creates unpredictable motion, like enemies in a game.
Customize It: Adjust random -240 to 240 to a smaller range (e.g., -100 to 100) or change Wait 1 second to 0.5 seconds.
Try It Yourself: Make a sprite glide to a random position using Glide 1 secs to x: y:.

Mini-Project: Catch the Star Game

Let's combine snippets to create a simple game where a player moves a sprite to catch a star and earn points. Create a new Scratch project with two sprites: a player (e.g., Scratch Cat) and a star (e.g., Star sprite).

```
// Player Sprite (e.g., Scratch Cat)
When green flag clicked
Set [score] to 0
Forever
    If [right arrow] key pressed
        Change X by 10
    If [left arrow] key pressed
        Change X by -10
    If [up arrow] key pressed
        Change Y by 10
    If [down arrow] key pressed
        Change Y by -10
    If touching [Star]
        Change [score] by 1
        Broadcast [newStar]

// Star Sprite
When green flag clicked
Forever
    Show
When I receive [newStar]
    Go to x: [random -240 to 240] y: [random -180 to 180]
    Play sound [pop] until done
```

How It Works:

- Uses Snippets 3 (key press), 5 (score), 7 (broadcast), and 8 (random movement).
- Player moves with arrow keys to touch the star, earning points.
- When the star is touched, it moves to a random position and plays a sound.
- Run by clicking the green flag in Scratch.

Try It Yourself: Add a costume switch (Snippet 2) to the star when it's caught or a backdrop change when the score reaches 5.

Debugging Tips

Scratch errors are often visual, but here's how to fix common issues:

- **Sprite Doesn't Move**: Check if "Motion" blocks (e.g., Move 10 steps) are inside a Forever loop or triggered by an event like When green flag clicked.
- **No Sound Plays**: Ensure the sound is added in the "Sounds" tab and matches the block (e.g., Play sound [pop]). Test by clicking the sound in the editor.
- **Score Not Updating**: Verify the score variable is created and the If touching [Sprite] condition references the correct sprite.
- **Blocks Not Running**: Ensure blocks are connected to an event (e.g., When green flag clicked) and not loose in the scripts area.

Tip: Click individual blocks to test them or use the "Variables" tab to watch score changes live.

What's Next?

You now have 8 reusable Scratch snippets for creating games and animations, plus a fun Catch the Star game to practice them. Experiment by tweaking snippets (e.g., add more key controls or sounds). In Chapter 9, we'll explore Java snippets for building apps, bridging visual coding to text-based programming. Keep your Scratch project open, and let's keep creating!

Chapter 9: Arrow Operators and Modern Symbols

The Evolution of Programming Symbols

Programming languages are living things that evolve over time. As programmers discovered better ways to express complex ideas, new symbols emerged. Arrow operators are some of the newest additions to programming languages, and they represent a shift toward more expressive, functional programming styles.

When I first saw symbols like `->`, `=>`, and `::`, I was completely baffled. They looked like emoticons or ASCII art, not legitimate programming symbols. But once I learned what they do, I realized they make code much more readable and elegant. These modern symbols let you write in a style that's closer to mathematical notation and natural language.

In this chapter, we'll explore these modern symbols, understand their different meanings across languages, and learn when and how to use them to write cleaner, more expressive code.

Arrow Functions (=>) - The Lambda Makers

The fat arrow `=>` is probably the most recognizable modern programming symbol. It creates anonymous functions (functions without names) in a concise way.

JavaScript Arrow Functions

javascript

```
// Traditional function
function double(x) {
  return x * 2;
}

// Arrow function - much shorter!
const double = x => x * 2;
```

```javascript
// Multiple parameters need parentheses
const add = (a, b) => a + b;

// Complex functions use braces
const processUser = user => {
  console.log(`Processing ${user.name}`);
  return user.name.toUpperCase();
};
```

Why Arrow Functions Matter

Before arrows (verbose and repetitive):

javascript

```javascript
const numbers = [1, 2, 3, 4, 5];

const doubled = numbers.map(function(num) {
  return num * 2;
});

const evens = numbers.filter(function(num) {
  return num % 2 === 0;
});
```

With arrows (clean and concise):

javascript

```javascript
const numbers = [1, 2, 3, 4, 5];

const doubled = numbers.map(num => num * 2);
const evens = numbers.filter(num => num % 2 === 0);
```

Python Lambda Functions

Python uses `lambda` keyword, but the concept is similar:

python

```python
# Traditional function
def double(x):
  return x * 2
```

```
# Lambda function (anonymous)
double = lambda x: x * 2

# Used with map, filter, etc.
numbers = [1, 2, 3, 4, 5]
doubled = list(map(lambda x: x * 2, numbers))
evens = list(filter(lambda x: x % 2 == 0, numbers))
```

C# Lambda Expressions

csharp

```
// C# uses => for lambda expressions
var numbers = new[] { 1, 2, 3, 4, 5 };

var doubled = numbers.Select(x => x * 2);
var evens = numbers.Where(x => x % 2 == 0);

// More complex lambdas
var users = GetUsers();
var adults = users.Where(user => user.Age >= 18)
          .Select(user => new { user.Name, user.Age });
```

Object Access Arrows (->) - The Pointer Dereferencers

The thin arrow -> has different meanings depending on the programming language, but it's most commonly associated with accessing members through pointers or references.

C++ Pointer Member Access

cpp

```
// C++ - accessing object members through pointers
struct Person {
  string name;
  int age;
  void greet() { cout << "Hello, I'm " << name; }
};

Person* personPtr = new Person{"Alice", 30};
```

```
// Using -> to access members through pointer
cout << personPtr->name;   // "Alice"
cout << personPtr->age;    // 30
personPtr->greet();        // "Hello, I'm Alice"

// Equivalent to (*personPtr).name, but much cleaner
cout << (*personPtr).name; // Same as above, but verbose
```

PHP Object Access

php

```
// PHP uses -> for object property and method access
class Person {
  public $name;
  public $age;

  public function greet() {
    return "Hello, I'm " . $this->name;
  }
}

$person = new Person();
$person->name = "Alice";
$person->age = 30;
echo $person->greet(); // "Hello, I'm Alice"
```

Rust Pattern Matching

rust

```
// Rust uses -> in match expressions and function signatures
fn process_result(result: Result<i32, String>) -> String {
  match result {
    Ok(value) => format!("Success: {}", value),
    Err(error) => format!("Error: {}", error),
  }
}

// Function return type annotation
```

```
fn calculate_tax(price: f64) -> f64 {
    price * 0.08
}
```

Scope Resolution (::) - The Namespace Navigators

The double colon :: helps you access things that are defined in specific namespaces, modules, or classes.

C++ Namespace Access

cpp

```cpp
// C++ namespaces and scope resolution
namespace Math {
    const double PI = 3.14159;
    double square(double x) { return x * x; }
}

namespace Graphics {
    const double PI = 3.14; // Different PI value
    void drawCircle(double radius) { /* ... */ }
}

// Using :: to specify which PI you want
double area = Math::PI * radius * radius;
Graphics::drawCircle(5.0);

// Global scope resolution
int globalVar = 100;
void someFunction() {
    int globalVar = 50;    // Local variable shadows global
    cout << ::globalVar;   // Access global version (100)
    cout << globalVar;     // Access local version (50)
}
```

Rust Module Access

rust

```rust
// Rust modules and paths
mod math {
```

```
    pub const PI: f64 = 3.14159;
    pub fn square(x: f64) -> f64 { x * x }
}

mod graphics {
    pub const PI: f64 = 3.14;
    pub fn draw_circle(radius: f64) { /* ... */ }
}

// Using :: to access module items
let area = math::PI * radius * radius;
graphics::draw_circle(5.0);

// Standard library access
let numbers = vec![1, 2, 3];
let max_value = std::cmp::max(10, 20);
```

Python Class Methods and Static Access

python

```
# Python uses . but the concept is similar
class MathUtils:
    PI = 3.14159

    @staticmethod
    def square(x):
        return x * x

    @classmethod
    def circle_area(cls, radius):
        return cls.PI * radius * radius

# Accessing static members
area = MathUtils.circle_area(5)
squared = MathUtils.square(4)
```

Nullish Coalescing (??) - The Default Providers

The nullish coalescing operator provides default values when dealing with null or undefined values.

JavaScript Nullish Coalescing

javascript

```javascript
// ?? provides defaults for null or undefined (but not other falsy values)
let username = user.name ?? "Anonymous";
let port = config.port ?? 3000;
let theme = settings.theme ?? "light";

// Different from || operator:
let count1 = 0;
let result1 = count1 || 10;  // 10 (0 is falsy)
let result2 = count1 ?? 10;  // 0 (0 is not null/undefined)

// Chaining for nested properties
let city = user?.profile?.address?.city ?? "Unknown";
```

C# Null Coalescing

csharp

```csharp
// C# has had ?? for much longer
string username = user.Name ?? "Anonymous";
int port = config.Port ?? 3000;

// Null coalescing assignment (??=)
username ??= "DefaultUser"; // Only assign if username is null
```

Optional Chaining (?.) - The Safe Accessors

Optional chaining lets you safely access nested properties without worrying about null/undefined errors.

JavaScript Optional Chaining

javascript

```javascript
// Without optional chaining (verbose and error-prone)
let city;
if (user && user.profile && user.profile.address) {
  city = user.profile.address.city;
} else {
  city = undefined;
}
```

```
// With optional chaining (clean and safe)
let city = user?.profile?.address?.city;

// Works with methods too
let result = api?.getData?.();

// Array access
let firstItem = items?.[0];
let dynamicProperty = user?.[propertyName];
```

Swift Optional Chaining

swift

```
// Swift has similar optional chaining
class Person {
  var address: Address?
}

class Address {
  var city: String?
}

let person = Person()
let city = person.address?.city // Returns nil if address is nil
```

Spread and Rest Operators (...) - The Collectors and Distributors

The three dots ... have multiple uses in modern programming languages.

JavaScript Spread Operator

javascript

```
// Spread arrays
let numbers1 = [1, 2, 3];
let numbers2 = [4, 5, 6];
let combined = [...numbers1, ...numbers2]; // [1, 2, 3, 4, 5, 6]

// Spread objects
let person = { name: "Alice", age: 30 };
```

```javascript
let employee = { ...person, job: "Developer" };
// { name: "Alice", age: 30, job: "Developer" }

// Function calls
function sum(a, b, c) {
  return a + b + c;
}
let nums = [1, 2, 3];
let total = sum(...nums); // Same as sum(1, 2, 3)
```

JavaScript Rest Parameters

javascript

```javascript
// Rest parameters - collect remaining arguments
function sum(first, ...rest) {
  console.log("First:", first);  // 1
  console.log("Rest:", rest);    // [2, 3, 4, 5]
  return rest.reduce((acc, num) => acc + num, first);
}

sum(1, 2, 3, 4, 5);

// Destructuring with rest
let [first, second, ...remaining] = [1, 2, 3, 4, 5];
console.log(first);     // 1
console.log(second);    // 2
console.log(remaining); // [3, 4, 5]
```

Python Unpacking

python

```python
# Python uses * for similar functionality
numbers1 = [1, 2, 3]
numbers2 = [4, 5, 6]
combined = [*numbers1, *numbers2]  # [1, 2, 3, 4, 5, 6]

# Function arguments
def greet(name, *args, **kwargs):
  print(f"Hello {name}")
  print(f"Additional args: {args}")
```

```
    print(f"Keyword args: {kwargs}")

greet("Alice", "extra", "info", age=30, city="NYC")
```

Template Literals and String Interpolation

Modern languages provide better ways to build strings with embedded values.

JavaScript Template Literals

javascript

```
// Template literals with backticks
let name = "Alice";
let age = 25;
let message = `Hello, my name is ${name} and I am ${age} years old.`;

// Multi-line strings
let html = `
<div class="user">
  <h2>${name}</h2>
  <p>Age: ${age}</p>
</div>
`;

// Expression evaluation
let price = 19.99;
let tax = 0.08;
let receipt = `Total: $${(price * (1 + tax)).toFixed(2)}`;
```

Python f-strings

python

```
# Python f-strings (Python 3.6+)
name = "Alice"
age = 30
message = f"Hello, my name is {name} and I am {age} years old."

# Expression evaluation
price = 19.99
tax = 0.08
```

```
receipt = f"Total: ${price * (1 + tax):.2f}"

# Multi-line f-strings
html = f"""
<div class="user">
  <h2>{name}</h2>
  <p>Age: {age}</p>
</div>
"""
```

Practical Exercises

Exercise 1: Arrow Function Conversion

javascript

```javascript
// Convert these traditional functions to arrow functions
function square(x) {
  return x * x;
}

function isEven(num) {
  return num % 2 === 0;
}

function greetUser(name) {
  console.log(`Hello, ${name}!`);
  return `Greeting sent to ${name}`;
}

// Solutions:
const square = x => x * x;
const isEven = num => num % 2 === 0;
const greetUser = name => {
  console.log(`Hello, ${name}!`);
  return `Greeting sent to ${name}`;
};

// Test them
console.log(square(5));     // 25
```

```javascript
console.log(isEven(4));      // true
console.log(greetUser("Alice")); // "Greeting sent to Alice"
```

Exercise 2: Safe Property Access

javascript

```javascript
// Practice with optional chaining and nullish coalescing
let users = [
  {
    name: "Alice",
    profile: {
      address: {
        city: "New York",
        zip: "10001"
      }
    }
  },
  {
    name: "Bob",
    profile: {
      // No address
    }
  },
  {
    name: "Charlie"
    // No profile
  }
];

// Your task: safely extract city information for each user
users.forEach(user => {
  let city = user?.profile?.address?.city ?? "City Unknown";
  let zip = user?.profile?.address?.zip ?? "ZIP Unknown";

  console.log(`${user.name}: ${city}, ${zip}`);
});
```

```
// Expected output:
// Alice: New York, 10001
// Bob: City Unknown, ZIP Unknown
// Charlie: City Unknown, ZIP Unknown
```

Exercise 3: Data Processing Pipeline

javascript

```javascript
// Create a data processing pipeline using modern operators
let salesData = [
  { product: "Laptop", price: 999, quantity: 2, category: "Electronics" },
  { product: "Mouse", price: 25, quantity: 5, category: "Electronics" },
  { product: "Book", price: 15, quantity: 3, category: "Books" },
  { product: "Phone", price: 699, quantity: 1, category: "Electronics" },
  { product: "Notebook", price: 5, quantity: 10, category: "Books" }
];

// Your task: Use arrow functions and array methods to:
// 1. Calculate total value for each item (price * quantity)
// 2. Filter for items worth more than $50
// 3. Group by category
// 4. Calculate category totals

// Solution:
const processedData = salesData
  .map(item => ({
    ...item,
    totalValue: item.price * item.quantity
  }))
  .filter(item => item.totalValue > 50)
  .reduce((acc, item) => {
    const category = item.category;
    if (!acc[category]) {
      acc[category] = { items: [], total: 0 };
    }
    acc[category].items.push(item);
    acc[category].total += item.totalValue;
    return acc;
  }, {});
```

```
console.log(processedData);
```

Modern Symbols in Different Languages

JavaScript:

```javascript
const double = x => x * 2;          // Arrow function
const city = user?.address?.city;   // Optional chaining
const name = user.name ?? "Unknown"; // Nullish coalescing
const combined = [...arr1, ...arr2]; // Spread operator
```

C++:

```cpp
person->getName();             // Pointer member access
Math::PI;                    // Namespace access
auto lambda = [](int x) { return x * 2; }; // Lambda function
```

Python:

```python
result = lambda x: x * 2        # Lambda function
message = f"Hello {name}!"       # f-string interpolation
combined = [*list1, *list2]      # Unpacking
```

Rust:

```rust
let result = numbers.iter()       // Method chaining
  .filter(|&x| x > 0)         // Closure
  .map(|&x| x * 2)            // Another closure
  .collect::<Vec<_>>();        // Turbofish operator ::< >
```

Key Takeaways

Modern programming symbols make code more expressive and concise:

1. **Arrow functions (=>)** create anonymous functions with cleaner syntax
2. **Object access arrows (->)** dereference pointers and access object members
3. **Scope resolution (::)** navigates namespaces and modules
4. **Nullish coalescing (??)** provides safe default values
5. **Optional chaining (?.)** prevents null/undefined errors

6. **Spread/Rest (...)** collect and distribute array/object elements
7. **Template literals** enable string interpolation with embedded expressions

These modern symbols represent the evolution of programming languages toward more functional, expressive styles. While they might seem intimidating at first, they actually make code more readable and less prone to errors once you understand them.

Understanding these symbols prepares you for modern codebases and helps you write cleaner, more maintainable code. They're not just syntactic sugar—they represent fundamental shifts in how we think about programming problems.

Chapter 10: Java: Snippets for Building Robust Applications

Welcome to Java, a powerful and versatile programming language used for everything from mobile apps to enterprise systems! Java's clear syntax and strong structure make it great for beginners learning to build reliable applications. In this chapter, you'll learn 8 reusable Java snippets for common tasks like looping, handling arrays, and reading input. We'll also build a mini-project to combine these snippets and share tips for fixing common errors. Whether you're new to coding or ready to create your first app, these snippets will help you get started with Java. Let's dive in!

Why Java?

Java is beginner-friendly yet robust, running on billions of devices worldwide. Its "write once, run anywhere" philosophy ensures your code works across platforms, from desktops to Android phones. Java's reusable methods and classes align perfectly with this book's focus on snippets, and its popularity in 2025 makes it a valuable skill for app development. Java pairs well with SQL (Chapter 7) for database-driven apps or Scratch (Chapter 8) for transitioning from visual to text-based coding. If you haven't set up a Java environment, check Chapter 2 for a guide to installing the Java Development Kit (JDK) and Visual Studio Code (VS Code) with the Java Extension Pack. Ready? Create a file called App.java in your CodingProjects folder, and let's code!

Setup Recap

1. Install JDK (e.g., OpenJDK from adoptium.net) and VS Code with the Java Extension Pack.
2. Create a new file App.java in CodingProjects.
3. Use this template for snippets:

```
public class App {
    public static void main(String[] args) {
        // Paste snippet code here
    }
}
```

4. Run code in VS Code (use the “Run” button) or via terminal: javac App.java then java App.
5. Test snippets in an online IDE like replit.com if you prefer.

Snippet 1: Print a Greeting

This snippet prints a personalized message to the console.

```
System.out.println("Hello, " + name + "!");
```

Why It’s Useful: Displays output, like greetings or status messages, in any Java app.
Customize It: Replace name with a variable (e.g., String name = "Alice";) or use System.out.printf("Hello, %s!\n", name); for formatted output.
Setup: Add inside main method.
Try It Yourself: Print “Welcome, [your name]!” to the console.

Snippet 2: Loop Through Numbers

This snippet loops through a range of numbers.

```
for (int i = 1; i <= 5; i++) {
    System.out.println(i);
}
```

Why It’s Useful: Repeats tasks, like printing numbers or processing lists.
Customize It: Change 5 to 10 or use i += 2 for even numbers.
Output: Prints 1, 2, 3, 4, 5 (one per line).
Try It Yourself: Loop from 10 to 1 in reverse.

Snippet 3: Read User Input

This snippet reads a string from the console.

```
import java.util.Scanner;

Scanner scanner = new Scanner(System.in);
System.out.print("Enter your name: ");
String name = scanner.nextLine();
System.out.println("You entered: " + name);
```

Why It’s Useful: Captures user input, like names or choices, for interactive apps.
Customize It: Use scanner.nextInt() for numbers or add a prompt like “Enter your age:”.
Setup: Add import java.util.Scanner; at the file’s top.
Try It Yourself: Read and print a user’s age as a number.

Snippet 4: Check Conditions

This snippet checks if a number is positive, negative, or zero.

```
int number = 10;
```

```
if (number > 0) {
    System.out.println("Positive");
} else if (number < 0) {
    System.out.println("Negative");
} else {
    System.out.println("Zero");
}
```

Why It's Useful: Makes decisions, like validating input or determining outcomes.
Customize It: Change number to a variable from user input (Snippet 3) or add more conditions.
Try It Yourself: Check if a number is even or odd (use number % 2 == 0).

Snippet 5: Create an Array

This snippet creates and prints an array of strings.

```
String[] fruits = {"Apple", "Banana", "Orange"};
for (String fruit : fruits) {
    System.out.println(fruit);
}
```

Why It's Useful: Stores and processes lists, like items or names, in apps.
Customize It: Use int[] numbers = {1, 2, 3}; for numbers or access a specific index (e.g., fruits[0]).
Output: Prints Apple, Banana, Orange (one per line).
Try It Yourself: Create an array of 4 colors and print them.

Snippet 6: Simple Method

This snippet defines a method to calculate the square of a number.

```
public static int square(int num) {
    return num * num;
}
// Usage in main: System.out.println(square(5));
```

Why It's Useful: Reuses code for calculations, like areas or scores.
Customize It: Modify to calculate num * num * num for a cube or add parameters for other operations.
Output: square(5) prints 25.
Try It Yourself: Create a method to double a number.

Snippet 7: Handle Exceptions

This snippet safely handles division to avoid errors.

```
try {
    int result = 10 / number;
    System.out.println("Result: " + result);
} catch (ArithmeticException e) {
    System.out.println("Error: Cannot divide by zero");
```

```
}
```

Why It's Useful: Prevents crashes from errors like division by zero.
Customize It: Add catch (Exception e) for general errors or use with user input (Snippet 3).
Try It Yourself: Handle an array index error (e.g., fruits[10] from Snippet 5).

Snippet 8: Write to a File

This snippet writes text to a file.

```
import java.io.FileWriter;

try {
    FileWriter writer = new FileWriter("output.txt");
    writer.write("Hello, Java!");
    writer.close();
    System.out.println("File written successfully");
} catch (IOException e) {
    System.out.println("Error writing to file");
}
```

Why It's Useful: Saves data, like logs or user input, for later use.
Customize It: Append with new FileWriter("output.txt", true) or write multiple lines.
Setup: Add import java.io.FileWriter; and ensure file permissions.
Try It Yourself: Write a user's name (from Snippet 3) to a file.

Mini-Project: Simple To-Do List App

Let's combine snippets to create a console-based to-do list app. Create TodoApp.java:

```
import java.util.ArrayList;
import java.util.Scanner;

public class TodoApp {
    public static void main(String[] args) {
        ArrayList<String> tasks = new ArrayList<>();
        Scanner scanner = new Scanner(System.in);

        while (true) {
            System.out.println("\n1. Add Task\n2. View Tasks\n3. Exit");
            System.out.print("Choose an option: ");
            int choice = scanner.nextInt();
            scanner.nextLine(); // Clear buffer

            if (choice == 1) {
                System.out.print("Enter task: ");
                String task = scanner.nextLine();
                tasks.add(task);
                System.out.println("Task added!");
                try {
                    FileWriter writer = new FileWriter("tasks.txt", true);
                    writer.write(task + "\n");
                    writer.close();
                } catch (IOException e) {
                    System.out.println("Error saving task");
```

```
                }
            } else if (choice == 2) {
                if (tasks.isEmpty()) {
                    System.out.println("No tasks!");
                } else {
                    System.out.println("Tasks:");
                    for (int i = 0; i < tasks.size(); i++) {
                        System.out.println((i + 1) + ". " + tasks.get(i));
                    }
                }
            } else if (choice == 3) {
                System.out.println("Goodbye!");
                break;
            } else {
                System.out.println("Invalid choice");
            }
        }
        scanner.close();
    }
}
```

How It Works:

- Uses Snippets 3 (input), 5 (array, using ArrayList), 7 (exception handling), and 8 (file writing).
- Lets users add tasks to a list, view them, and save to tasks.txt.
- Run with javac TodoApp.java and java TodoApp in a terminal or VS Code.

Try It Yourself: Add an option to delete a task by index (e.g., tasks.remove(index)).

Debugging Tips

Java errors can be intimidating, but here's how to fix common ones:

- **"Cannot find symbol"**: Check variable/method names (e.g., scanner vs Scanner) or missing imports (e.g., java.util.Scanner). Case matters!
- **"NullPointerException"**: Ensure variables are initialized (e.g., String[] fruits = new String[3] before use). Check array indices.
- **"FileNotFoundException"**: Verify file paths for FileWriter or ensure write permissions. Use absolute paths if needed (e.g., C:/CodingProjects/tasks.txt).
- **No Output**: Confirm System.out.println is used and the main method is correct. Add print statements to trace code flow.

Tip: Use VS Code's debugger or add System.out.println("Step X"); to track where code fails.

What's Next?

You now have 8 reusable Java snippets for building applications, plus a to-do list app to practice them. Experiment by tweaking snippets (e.g., add more menu options or read from a file). In Chapter 10, we'll explore C# snippets, which share similarities with Java for building apps. Keep your CodingProjects folder ready, and let's keep coding!

Chapter 11: C#: Snippets for Versatile App Development

Welcome to C#, a modern and versatile programming language used for building apps, games, and web services! C# is beginner-friendly with clear syntax, making it ideal for creating robust applications, from desktop tools to Unity games. In this chapter, you'll learn 8 reusable C# snippets for tasks like looping, handling lists, and reading input. We'll also build a mini-project to combine these snippets and share tips for fixing common errors. Whether you're new to coding or transitioning from Java (Chapter 9), these snippets will help you create powerful apps. Let's get started with C#!

Why C#?

C# (pronounced "C-sharp") is developed by Microsoft and combines Java's structure with beginner-friendly features. It runs on Windows, macOS, and Linux, powering apps like desktop tools, mobile apps, and games in Unity. Its reusable methods and classes align perfectly with this book's focus on snippets, and its popularity in 2025 makes it a valuable skill for app development. C# pairs well with SQL (Chapter 7) for database apps or Scratch (Chapter 8) for moving from visual to text-based coding. If you haven't set up a C# environment, check Chapter 2 for a guide to installing .NET SDK and Visual Studio Code (VS Code) with the C# extension. Ready? Create a file called App.cs in your CodingProjects folder, and let's code!

Setup Recap

1. Install .NET SDK from dotnet.microsoft.com and VS Code with the C# extension by Microsoft.
2. Create a new file App.cs in CodingProjects.
3. Use this template for snippets:

```
using System;

class Program {
    static void Main(string[] args) {
        // Paste snippet code here
    }
}
```

4. Run code in VS Code (use the "Run" button) or via terminal: dotnet new console -o MyApp, add code to Program.cs, then dotnet run.
5. Test snippets in an online IDE like replit.com if preferred.

Snippet 1: Print a Greeting

This snippet prints a personalized message to the console.

```
string name = "Alice";
Console.WriteLine($"Hello, {name}!");
```

Why It's Useful: Displays output, like greetings or status messages, in any C# app.
Customize It: Replace name with user input (see Snippet 3) or use Console.Write for inline output without a newline.
Output: Prints "Hello, Alice!".
Try It Yourself: Print "Welcome, [your name]!" to the console.

Snippet 2: Loop Through Numbers

This snippet loops through a range of numbers.

```
for (int i = 1; i <= 5; i++) {
    Console.WriteLine(i);
}
```

Why It's Useful: Repeats tasks, like printing numbers or processing data.
Customize It: Change 5 to 10 or use i += 2 for even numbers.
Output: Prints 1, 2, 3, 4, 5 (one per line).
Try It Yourself: Loop from 10 to 1 in reverse.

Snippet 3: Read User Input

This snippet reads a string from the console.

```
Console.Write("Enter your name: ");
string name = Console.ReadLine();
Console.WriteLine($"You entered: {name}");
```

Why It's Useful: Captures user input, like names or choices, for interactive apps.
Customize It: Use int.Parse(Console.ReadLine()) for numbers or add a prompt like "Enter your age:".
Setup: Ensure using System; is included.
Try It Yourself: Read and print a user's age as a number.

Snippet 4: Check Conditions

This snippet checks if a number is positive, negative, or zero.

```
int number = 10;
if (number > 0) {
    Console.WriteLine("Positive");
} else if (number < 0) {
    Console.WriteLine("Negative");
} else {
    Console.WriteLine("Zero");
}
```

Why It's Useful: Makes decisions, like validating input or determining outcomes.
Customize It: Use with user input (Snippet 3) or check if a number is even (number % 2 == 0).
Try It Yourself: Check if a number is divisible by 3.

Snippet 5: Create a List

This snippet creates and prints a list of strings.

```
using System.Collections.Generic;

List<string> fruits = new List<string> { "Apple", "Banana", "Orange" };
foreach (string fruit in fruits) {
    Console.WriteLine(fruit);
}
```

Why It's Useful: Stores and processes dynamic lists, like items or tasks.
Customize It: Use List<int> for numbers or add items with fruits.Add("Mango").
Setup: Add using System.Collections.Generic;.
Output: Prints Apple, Banana, Orange (one per line).
Try It Yourself: Create a list of 4 colors and print them.

Snippet 6: Simple Method

This snippet defines a method to calculate the square of a number.

```
static int Square(int num) {
    return num * num;
}
// Usage in Main: Console.WriteLine(Square(5));
```

Why It's Useful: Reuses code for calculations, like areas or scores.
Customize It: Modify to calculate num * num * num for a cube or add parameters for other operations.
Output: Square(5) prints 25.
Try It Yourself: Create a method to triple a number.

Snippet 7: Handle Exceptions

This snippet safely handles division to avoid errors.

```
try {
    int number = 10;
    int divisor = 0;
    int result = number / divisor;
    Console.WriteLine($"Result: {result}");
} catch (DivideByZeroException) {
    Console.WriteLine("Error: Cannot divide by zero");
}
```

Why It's Useful: Prevents crashes from errors like division by zero.
Customize It: Use with user input (Snippet 3) or catch other exceptions like FormatException for invalid input.
Try It Yourself: Handle an invalid number input (e.g., int.Parse).

Snippet 8: Write to a File

This snippet writes text to a file.

```
using System.IO;

try {
    File.WriteAllText("output.txt", "Hello, C#!");
    Console.WriteLine("File written successfully");
} catch (IOException) {
    Console.WriteLine("Error writing to file");
}
```

Why It's Useful: Saves data, like logs or user input, for later use.
Customize It: Append with File.AppendAllText or write multiple lines with File.WriteAllLines.
Setup: Add using System.IO;.
Try It Yourself: Write a user's name (from Snippet 3) to a file.

Mini-Project: Simple Shopping List App

Let's combine snippets to create a console-based shopping list app. Create ShoppingList.cs:

```
using System;
using System.Collections.Generic;
using System.IO;

class ShoppingList {
    static void Main(string[] args) {
        List<string> items = new List<string>();

        while (true) {
            Console.WriteLine("\n1. Add Item\n2. View Items\n3. Save and
Exit");
            Console.Write("Choose an option: ");
            string input = Console.ReadLine();

            try {
                int choice = int.Parse(input);

                if (choice == 1) {
                    Console.Write("Enter item: ");
                    string item = Console.ReadLine();
                    items.Add(item);
                    Console.WriteLine("Item added!");
                } else if (choice == 2) {
                    if (items.Count == 0) {
                        Console.WriteLine("No items!");
                    } else {
                        Console.WriteLine("Shopping List:");
                        for (int i = 0; i < items.Count; i++) {
                            Console.WriteLine($"{i + 1}. {items[i]}");
                        }
                    }
                } else if (choice == 3) {
                    try {
                        File.WriteAllLines("shopping.txt", items);
                        Console.WriteLine("List saved to shopping.txt!");
```

```
                        break;
                    } catch (IOException) {
                        Console.WriteLine("Error saving list");
                    }
                } else {
                    Console.WriteLine("Invalid choice");
                }
            } catch (FormatException) {
                Console.WriteLine("Please enter a number");
            }
        }
    }
}
```

How It Works:

- Uses Snippets 3 (input), 5 (list), 7 (exception handling), and 8 (file writing).
- Lets users add items to a shopping list, view them, and save to shopping.txt.
- Run with dotnet run in a terminal or VS Code.

Try It Yourself: Add an option to remove an item by index (e.g., items.RemoveAt(index)).

Debugging Tips

C# errors can seem complex, but here's how to fix common ones:

- **"CS0103: Name does not exist"**: Check variable/method names (e.g., Console vs console) or missing imports (e.g., using System.IO;). Case matters!
- **"NullReferenceException"**: Ensure variables are initialized (e.g., List<string> items = new List<string>();) before use. Check list indices.
- **"IOException"**: Verify file paths for File.WriteAllText or ensure write permissions. Use absolute paths if needed (e.g., C:/CodingProjects/shopping.txt).
- **No Output**: Confirm Console.WriteLine is used and the Main method is correct. Add Console.WriteLine("Step X"); to trace code flow.

Tip: Use VS Code's debugger or add Console.WriteLine statements to track where code fails.

What's Next?

You now have 8 reusable C# snippets for building applications, plus a shopping list app to practice them. Experiment by tweaking snippets (e.g., add more menu options or read from a file). In Chapter 11, we'll explore R snippets for data analysis, perfect for visualizing data. Keep your CodingProjects folder ready, and let's keep coding!

Chapter 12: TypeScript: Snippets for Modern Web Development

Welcome to TypeScript, a powerful language that adds types to JavaScript, making web development more reliable and fun! TypeScript is perfect for beginners who want to build modern web apps with fewer errors, combining JavaScript's flexibility with type safety. In this chapter, you'll learn 8 reusable TypeScript snippets for tasks like defining types, creating functions, and building React components. We'll also create a mini-project to combine these snippets and share tips for fixing common issues. Whether you're enhancing a website from Chapters 5–6 or starting fresh, these snippets will level up your web projects. Let's dive into TypeScript!

Why TypeScript?

TypeScript, developed by Microsoft, extends JavaScript (Chapter 4) with types, catching errors early and improving code clarity. It's widely used in 2025 for web apps, especially with frameworks like React, Angular, and Vue. Its reusable functions and components align with this book's focus on snippets, and it pairs well with HTML/CSS (Chapters 5–6) for styling and SQL (Chapter 7) for data-driven apps. If you haven't set up TypeScript, check Chapter 2 for a guide to installing Node.js, Visual Studio Code (VS Code), and the TypeScript extension. Ready? Create a new project, and let's code!

Setup Recap

1. Install Node.js from nodejs.org and VS Code with the TypeScript extension.
2. Create a folder ts-project in CodingProjects, run npm init -y, then npm install typescript --save-dev.
3. Initialize TypeScript: npx tsc --init to create tsconfig.json.
4. Create a file app.ts for snippets or index.tsx for React snippets.
5. Run snippets with npx tsc app.ts && node app.js or use an online IDE like replit.com.
6. For React, run npx create-react-app my-app --template typescript, then edit src/App.tsx.
7. Use this template for core TypeScript snippets:

```
console.log("Hello, TypeScript!");
```

For React snippets, use:

```
import React from 'react';
const App: React.FC = () => {
  return <div>Hello, React!</div>;
};
export default App;
```

Snippet 1: Define a Type

This snippet creates a type for structured data.

```
type User = {
  name: string;
  age: number;
};
const user: User = { name: "Alice", age: 25 };
console.log(`Hello, ${user.name}! Age: ${user.age}`);
```

Why It's Useful: Ensures data has the correct shape, like user profiles, preventing errors.
Customize It: Add fields like email: string or use interface User instead of type.
Output: Prints "Hello, Alice! Age: 25".
Try It Yourself: Create a type for a book with title and year.

Snippet 2: Type-Safe Function

This snippet defines a function with typed parameters and return value.

```
function add(a: number, b: number): number {
  return a + b;
}
console.log(add(5, 3));
```

Why It's Useful: Prevents incorrect inputs (e.g., strings) and ensures return types.
Customize It: Change to multiply (a * b) or return string for formatted output.
Output: Prints 8.
Try It Yourself: Create a function to subtract two numbers.

Snippet 3: Array of Typed Objects

This snippet creates an array of typed objects.

```
type Item = { name: string; price: number };
const items: Item[] = [
  { name: "Apple", price: 1.5 },
  { name: "Banana", price: 0.75 }
];
items.forEach(item => console.log(`${item.name}: $${item.price}`));
```

Why It's Useful: Manages lists, like products or tasks, with type safety.
Customize It: Add fields like quantity: number or filter with items.filter(item => item.price > 1).
Output: Prints "Apple: $1.5", "Banana: $0.75".
Try It Yourself: Create an array of 3 books with title and price.

Snippet 4: Optional Parameters

This snippet uses optional parameters in a function.

```
function greet(name: string, greeting?: string): string {
  return `${greeting || "Hello"}, ${name}!`;
}
console.log(greet("Bob"));
console.log(greet("Bob", "Hi"));
```

Why It's Useful: Allows flexible function calls, like optional greetings.
Customize It: Add more optional parameters or use a default value (e.g., greeting: string = "Hello").
Output: Prints "Hello, Bob!", "Hi, Bob!".
Try It Yourself: Create a function with an optional age parameter.

Snippet 5: React Component with Props

This snippet creates a React component with typed props.

```
import React from 'react';

type Props = {
  title: string;
};
const Header: React.FC<Props> = ({ title }) => {
  return <h1>{title}</h1>;
};
export default Header;
// Usage: <Header title="My App" />
```

Why It's Useful: Builds reusable UI components with type safety for web apps.
Customize It: Add props like color: string or use defaultProps.
Setup: Use in src/App.tsx in a React project.
Try It Yourself: Create a component with a subtitle prop.

Snippet 6: Handle User Input

This snippet handles input in a React component.

```
import React, { useState } from 'react';

const InputForm: React.FC = () => {
  const [name, setName] = useState<string>("");
  return (
    <div>
      <input
        type="text"
        value={name}
        onChange={(e) => setName(e.target.value)}
        placeholder="Enter name"
      />
      <p>Hello, {name || "Guest"}!</p>
    </div>
  );
};
export default InputForm;
```

Why It's Useful: Captures user input, like form data, with type safety.
Customize It: Add a number input with useState<number>(0) or validate input.
Setup: Use in a React project.
Try It Yourself: Add a second input for age.

Snippet 7: Fetch Data with Types

This snippet fetches data with typed responses.

```
async function fetchUser(id: number): Promise<User> {
```

```
  const response = await
fetch(`https://jsonplaceholder.typicode.com/users/${id}`);
  const user: User = await response.json();
  return user;
}
// Usage
fetchUser(1).then(user => console.log(user.name));
```

Why It's Useful: Safely fetches data, like user profiles, for web apps.
Customize It: Change the endpoint or add error handling with try/catch.
Setup: Define type User = { name: string }.
Try It Yourself: Fetch a list of posts instead of users.

Snippet 8: Union Types

This snippet uses union types for flexible variables.

```
type Status = "success" | "error" | "loading";
let appStatus: Status = "loading";
console.log(`Status: ${appStatus}`);
```

Why It's Useful: Restricts variables to specific values, like app states.
Customize It: Add more statuses (e.g., "pending") or use in a function.
Output: Prints "Status: loading".
Try It Yourself: Create a function that prints a message based on Status.

Mini-Project: Task List React Component

Let's combine snippets to create a TypeScript React task list component. Create a new React project (npx create-react-app task-list --template typescript) and edit src/App.tsx:

```
import React, { useState } from 'react';
import './App.css';

type Task = {
  id: number;
  text: string;
  done: boolean;
};

const TaskList: React.FC = () => {
  const [tasks, setTasks] = useState<Task[]>([]);
  const [newTask, setNewTask] = useState<string>("");

  const addTask = () => {
    if (newTask) {
      setTasks([...tasks, { id: tasks.length + 1, text: newTask, done:
false }]);
      setNewTask("");
    }
  };

  return (
    <div className="container">
```

```
        <h1>Task List</h1>
        <input
          type="text"
          value={newTask}
          onChange={(e) => setNewTask(e.target.value)}
          placeholder="Add a task"
        />
        <button onClick={addTask}>Add</button>
        <ul>
          {tasks.map(task => (
            <li key={task.id}>{task.text} {task.done ? "(Done)" : ""}</li>
          ))}
        </ul>
      </div>
    );
};

export default TaskList;
```

Add src/App.css for styling (from Chapter 6):

```
.container {
  max-width: 600px;
  margin: 0 auto;
  padding: 20px;
}
button {
  background-color: #007bff;
  color: white;
  padding: 10px;
  border: none;
  cursor: pointer;
}
button:hover {
  background-color: #0056b3;
}
```

How It Works:

- Uses Snippets 1 (type), 3 (array), 5 (React component), and 6 (input) to create a task list app.
- Users add tasks via an input field, displayed in a list.
- Run with npm start in the project folder.

Try It Yourself: Add a button to toggle task.done and display "Done" status.

Debugging Tips

TypeScript errors can be tricky, but here's how to fix common ones:

- **"Cannot find module"**: Ensure imports are correct (e.g., import React from 'react') and run npm install for dependencies.
- **"Property does not exist"**: Check type definitions (e.g., User has name) or add missing fields to types.

- **“Type ‘x’ is not assignable”**: Verify variable types match (e.g., string vs number) or use union types (Snippet 8).
- **No Output in React**: Confirm components are exported (export default) and rendered in App.tsx. Check console for errors (F12).

Tip: Use VS Code’s TypeScript error hints or run npx tsc --watch to catch issues early.

What’s Next?

You now have 8 reusable TypeScript snippets for web development, plus a task list app to practice them. Experiment by tweaking snippets (e.g., add more props or fetch real data). In Chapter 13, we’ll combine skills from previous chapters to build larger projects. Keep your ts-project folder ready, and let’s keep building!

Chapter 13: Building Real Projects

Multi-Language Projects (e.g., Web Apps, Data Dashboards) Using Snippets

Introduction

By now, you’ve collected dozens of snippets—tiny, reusable blocks of code that solve small problems. In this chapter, we’ll take the next step: combining snippets across different programming languages to build **real, working projects** such as web applications, dashboards, and automation tools.
You’ll see how these small pieces, when organized correctly, become powerful building blocks for complete systems.

1. Understanding Multi-Language Projects

Modern applications rarely rely on one language alone. A web app, for example, might use:

- **HTML & CSS** for structure and design
- **JavaScript or Python** for interactivity
- **SQL** for managing databases
- **API snippets** for external data connections

By combining snippets written in different languages, you can build systems where each language contributes its strengths.

2. Planning Your Project Structure

Before writing a single line of code, outline your **snippet architecture**:

1. **Frontend Snippets** – user interface elements (HTML, CSS, JS)
2. **Backend Snippets** – logic, routes, and data processing (Python, Node.js, PHP, etc.)

3. **Database Snippets** – table creation, queries, or stored procedures (SQL)
4. **Integration Snippets** – APIs or automation flows connecting everything

Tip: Use folders or a naming system (like `frontend/`, `backend/`, `database/`) to keep your snippets organized. Label each snippet clearly so you can reuse them later.

3. Building a Simple Web App

Let's walk through a mini-project example using snippets.

Project Example: Personal To-Do Web App

Goal: Create a web app that lets users add, view, and delete tasks.

Languages Used:

- HTML/CSS → Structure & design
- JavaScript → Interactivity
- Python (Flask) → Backend server
- SQLite → Database storage

Step 1 – HTML Snippet (User Interface)

```
<form id="taskForm">
  <input type="text" id="task" placeholder="Add a new task">
  <button type="submit">Add</button>
</form>
<ul id="taskList"></ul>
```

Step 2 – JavaScript Snippet (Frontend Logic)

```
document.getElementById('taskForm').onsubmit = async (e) => {
  e.preventDefault();
  const task = document.getElementById('task').value;
  await fetch('/add', {
    method: 'POST',
    body: JSON.stringify({ task }),
    headers: { 'Content-Type': 'application/json' }
  });
  location.reload();
};
```

Step 3 – Python Snippet (Backend Server)

```
from flask import Flask, request, jsonify
app = Flask(__name__)
tasks = []

@app.route('/add', methods=['POST'])
def add_task():
    data = request.get_json()
    tasks.append(data['task'])
```

```
    return jsonify({'status': 'added'})

@app.route('/tasks')
def get_tasks():
    return jsonify(tasks)

if __name__ == '__main__':
    app.run()
```

Each piece is reusable: the form snippet can fit in any HTML page, the JavaScript fetch call can be adapted to any API, and the Flask route can be extended for any backend.

4. Combining Snippets for Data Dashboards

Let's take another example—**a Data Dashboard** that visualizes information.

Languages Involved:

- **Python** → Data processing (using Pandas)
- **HTML/JavaScript** → Frontend display
- **Chart.js** → Visualization snippet

Python Snippet (Backend Data)

```
import pandas as pd
from flask import Flask, jsonify
app = Flask(__name__)

@app.route('/data')
def data():
    df = pd.read_csv('sales.csv')
    return jsonify(df.to_dict(orient='records'))
```

JavaScript Snippet (Frontend Chart)

```
fetch('/data')
  .then(res => res.json())
  .then(data => {
    const sales = data.map(d => d.amount);
    const labels = data.map(d => d.date);
    new Chart(document.getElementById('chart'), {
      type: 'line',
      data: { labels, datasets: [{ label: 'Sales', data: sales }] }
    });
  });
```

These snippets work together to deliver real-time visual insights. If you save each snippet properly, you can reuse the same dashboard structure for other data sources—just replace the CSV or API.

5. How to Integrate Snippets Across Languages

- **Use APIs as a bridge.** Python, PHP, or Node.js can expose data via endpoints.

- **Embed scripts dynamically.** Combine Python-generated HTML with embedded JavaScript snippets.
- **Use environment variables.** Keep your snippet-based systems secure and portable by storing credentials outside your code.
- **Automate the connections.** Use snippet automation tools like GitHub Gists, Visual Studio Code snippets, or custom JSON libraries to quickly pull code blocks into new projects.

6. Benefits of Multi-Language Snippet Projects

- Reuse tested code across different projects
- Save development time and reduce bugs
- Learn how multiple languages interact
- Build a library of modular building blocks for future ideas

7. Practice Projects for You

Try combining snippets to create:

1. **Weather App** – HTML + CSS + JS + OpenWeather API + Python backend
2. **Expense Tracker** – HTML + JS + SQL database + Flask or PHP backend
3. **AI-Powered Chat Interface** – JS frontend + Python backend + OpenAI API snippet
4. **Portfolio Website** – HTML + CSS snippets + embedded YouTube or image gallery snippet

Each of these reinforces your ability to integrate code, connect systems, and see how snippets make big ideas manageable.

8. Final Thoughts

When you start combining snippets across languages, you're not just writing code—you're **engineering solutions**. You're turning small ideas into real, working systems by recycling code intelligently.
That's the beauty of snippets: once you master reuse, you'll never have to start from scratch again.

AI Glossary — Letter A

Activation Function

A key part of neural networks that decides whether a neuron should be "activated" or not. It helps the network handle complex patterns, turning raw numbers into meaningful signals during learning.

Algorithm

A step-by-step set of instructions that tells a computer how to solve a problem or perform a task. In AI, algorithms are the "recipes" that guide machines in recognizing patterns, learning from data, and making predictions.

Anomaly Detection

A technique used in AI to find unusual patterns or behaviors that don't fit expected data. It's commonly used in fraud detection, cybersecurity, and system monitoring to identify potential problems

Artificial Intelligence (AI)

The science of creating machines that can perform tasks that normally require human intelligence — such as understanding language, recognizing images, solving problems, or making decisions.

Artificial Neural Network (ANN)

A system inspired by how the human brain works, made up of layers of connected nodes (neurons). Each node processes information and passes it along, allowing the system to "learn" patterns from data.

Artificial General Intelligence (AGI)

A theoretical form of AI that would be able to understand, learn, and perform any intellectual task a human can do. AGI doesn't exist yet, but it represents the ultimate goal of AI research — true human-like intelligence.

Artificial Narrow Intelligence (ANI)

AI designed for a specific task, such as language translation, facial recognition, or driving a car. Most AI today is narrow — powerful at one thing, but unable to perform unrelated tasks.

Attention Mechanism

A method used in advanced AI models (like transformers) that allows the system to focus on the most relevant parts of the input. It helps the AI "pay attention" to important words or data points when generating responses.

Augmented Intelligence

AI systems designed not to replace humans, but to assist them. Augmented intelligence emphasizes collaboration — combining human creativity and judgment with machine speed and accuracy.

Autonomous System

A system that can operate, make decisions, or take actions without direct human control. Examples include self-driving cars, delivery drones, or robotic assistants that use AI to navigate and respond to their environment.

🔠 *AI Glossary — Letter B*

Backpropagation

A key learning process used in neural networks to adjust the model's internal settings (weights) based on the errors it makes. By "propagating" mistakes backward through the network, the AI learns to improve accuracy over time.

Batch Learning

A method where an AI model is trained on a complete dataset all at once, rather than learning continuously. It's efficient for large, static datasets but less adaptable to changing data over time.

Bayesian Network

A graphical model that represents the relationships between variables and their probabilities. It helps AI systems reason under uncertainty — for example, predicting the likelihood of an event based on known factors.

Behavioral Analytics

AI techniques that analyze user actions, preferences, or digital patterns to predict future behavior. Often used in marketing, fraud detection, and personalized recommendations.

Bias in AI

When an AI system produces unfair or unbalanced results due to biased data or flawed training methods. Bias can affect hiring systems, loan approvals, and facial recognition — making fairness testing essential in AI development.

Big Data

Extremely large and complex datasets that traditional computers can't easily process. AI tools use big data to learn patterns, make predictions, and uncover insights across industries like healthcare, finance, and marketing.

Binary Classification

A machine learning task where the AI must choose between two possible outcomes — such as "spam or not spam," "yes or no," or "disease or no disease." It's one of the most basic types of AI decision-making.

Bit

The smallest unit of digital data, representing a value of **0** or **1**. In AI and computing, bits form the foundation for all data processing, storage, and communication. Eight bits make up one **byte**, and together they represent everything from numbers and text to images and videos.

Bitwise Operation

A type of mathematical operation that works directly on the binary representation (bits) of data. Bitwise operators (such as AND, OR, XOR, and NOT) are used in AI programming to control low-level logic, optimize performance, and manipulate data efficiently.

Blockchain AI

The combination of blockchain (a secure, distributed ledger) and artificial intelligence to improve transparency, data security, and trust in AI-driven systems.

Bot

Short for "robot," a bot is a program that performs automated tasks. In AI, chatbots are designed to simulate human conversation, while other bots perform repetitive digital actions like data scraping or scheduling.

Brute Force Algorithm

A simple but computationally expensive problem-solving method that tries every possible solution until it finds the correct one. Though inefficient, it guarantees accuracy for small problems.

🔠 AI Glossary — Letter C

Chatbot

An AI-powered program designed to simulate human conversation through text or voice. Chatbots can answer questions, provide customer support, teach lessons, or help automate business communication using natural language processing.

Classification

A core machine learning task where AI assigns input data into specific categories or labels — such as identifying whether an email is "spam" or "not spam." Classification models are trained using labeled examples to recognize patterns.

Clustering

An unsupervised learning technique where AI groups similar pieces of data together based on shared characteristics. Unlike classification, clustering doesn't use labeled data — it helps uncover hidden patterns or natural groupings within datasets.

Cognitive Computing

A branch of AI that mimics human reasoning, perception, and decision-making. Cognitive systems analyze unstructured data, recognize language and emotions, and provide intelligent suggestions — much like how the human brain interprets information.

Computer Vision

A field of AI that enables machines to "see" and interpret visual information such as images or videos. Computer vision powers facial recognition, object detection, medical imaging, and autonomous vehicles.

Convolutional Neural Network (CNN)

A specialized type of neural network used primarily for image and video analysis. CNNs automatically detect visual features like edges, shapes, and textures, allowing machines to recognize objects or patterns with high accuracy.

Context Window

The range of text or tokens that a language model can "see" and use at one time to generate its response. A larger context window allows AI to remember more of the conversation, leading to better understanding and consistency.

Corpus

A large and structured collection of texts used to train or evaluate language models. In AI, a corpus provides the examples that teach the model how words and phrases are used in real-world contexts.

Cross-Validation

A model evaluation technique used in machine learning to test how well a model generalizes to new, unseen data. The dataset is divided into parts (folds), and the model is trained and tested multiple times to ensure accuracy and reliability.

Cybernetics

The interdisciplinary study of communication and control in both machines and living organisms. In AI, cybernetics explores feedback loops — how systems monitor and adjust their behavior to maintain balance and achieve goals.

🔠 AI Glossary — Letter D

Data Analytics

The process of examining, cleaning, and interpreting data to uncover useful information and patterns. In AI, data analytics helps models learn from real-world data to make predictions and informed decisions.

Data Labeling

The act of tagging or annotating raw data with meaningful labels — such as identifying images with "cat" or "dog." Labeled data is essential for training supervised machine learning models.

Data Mining

The practice of exploring large datasets to discover hidden patterns, trends, or relationships. AI-powered data mining helps businesses predict customer behavior, detect fraud, and improve decision-making.

Data Science

An interdisciplinary field that combines statistics, programming, and AI to extract insights from data. Data scientists build predictive models, analyze trends, and guide data-driven decisions.

Dataset

A structured collection of data used to train or test AI models. A dataset can include text, images, numbers, or audio. The quality and diversity of the dataset directly affect how well an AI performs.

Decision Tree

A visual and logical model used in AI for decision-making. Each branch represents a question or condition, and each leaf represents an outcome. Decision trees are popular for their simplicity and interpretability.

Deep Learning

A subset of machine learning that uses multi-layered neural networks to learn complex patterns. Deep learning powers technologies like voice recognition, autonomous driving, and image generation.

Dimensionality Reduction

A mathematical process used to simplify datasets by reducing the number of variables while preserving important information. It helps AI models work faster and more efficiently, especially with large data.

Domain Adaptation

A technique in AI that allows a model trained on one dataset to perform well on a different but related dataset. It helps AI generalize better to new environments or data types.

Drift Detection

The process of identifying when an AI model's performance declines because real-world data has changed. Detecting data drift ensures the model stays accurate and up-to-date over time.

AI Glossary — Letter E

E-book Recommendation Systems

AI algorithms that suggest books or reading materials based on user preferences, past selections, or browsing behavior. They enhance reading platforms by delivering personalized content to readers.

E-Brainstorming

The use of AI tools to assist with creative idea generation. E-brainstorming platforms help individuals and teams generate fresh perspectives, organize thoughts, and develop new solutions quickly.

E-commerce AI

AI applications that enhance online shopping experiences. These systems recommend products, predict customer behavior, optimize pricing, and improve inventory management for e-commerce platforms.

Edge AI

Artificial Intelligence that runs directly on local devices (like smartphones, cameras, or IoT sensors) instead of relying on cloud servers. Edge AI allows faster responses, improved privacy, and reduced internet dependency.

E-Learning AI

The use of AI in online education to personalize learning experiences, analyze student performance, and recommend tailored study materials. E-Learning AI helps teachers and learners adapt lessons to individual needs.

E-mail Filtering AI

AI systems that automatically detect and organize incoming emails — such as sorting spam, prioritizing important messages, or detecting phishing threats — using natural language and pattern recognition.

Embedding

A mathematical representation of data (like words, sentences, or images) in numerical form. In AI, embeddings help models understand meaning, context, and similarity — crucial for natural language processing and image recognition.

Emotion AI

Also called Affective Computing, it's a branch of AI that recognizes, interprets, and responds to human emotions using facial expressions, voice tones, or physiological signals. It's used in customer service, education, and healthcare.

Ensemble Learning

A technique that combines multiple AI models to produce stronger, more accurate results than a single model could achieve alone. Common ensemble methods include bagging, boosting, and stacking.

E-Transaction Security

AI-based systems that monitor and protect online financial transactions. They detect unusual activity, verify identities, and prevent fraud in digital banking and online payment systems.

🔠 AI Glossary — Letter F

Face Recognition AI

A technology that uses machine learning and computer vision to identify or verify a person's identity based on facial features. It's used in security systems, smartphones, and law enforcement, but also raises privacy and ethical concerns.

False Positive

A situation in which an AI system incorrectly identifies something as true when it's not. For example, a spam filter marking a legitimate email as spam. Reducing false positives improves reliability and user trust.

False Negative

The opposite of a false positive — when an AI system fails to identify something that is true. For example, a medical AI missing signs of a disease. Balancing false positives and negatives is vital in sensitive applications.

Feature Engineering

The process of creating, transforming, or selecting data features to improve machine learning model performance. It's a key step that combines human insight with data science techniques to optimize accuracy.

Feature Extraction

The process of identifying the most important characteristics or variables from raw data. In AI, feature extraction helps reduce complexity and improve model accuracy by focusing on relevant information.

Feature Map

In deep learning, particularly in convolutional neural networks (CNNs), a feature map represents visual patterns detected in an image. It helps the network recognize shapes, textures, and other important details.

Federated Learning

A training method that allows multiple devices or organizations to collaboratively train an AI model without sharing raw data. Each participant trains the model locally, and only updates are shared — improving data privacy and security.

Fine-Tuning

A process of retraining a pre-trained AI model on a smaller, specific dataset to make it more accurate for a particular task. Fine-tuning allows developers to customize general-purpose models for specialized applications.

Forecasting Model

An AI system that predicts future events or trends based on historical data. Forecasting models are widely used in business, weather prediction, finance, and supply chain management.

Fuzzy Logic

An AI reasoning system that allows for partial truths rather than strict "true or false" decisions. It's useful for handling uncertainty in real-world situations like temperature control, medical diagnosis, and robotics.

🔤 AI Glossary — Letter G

GAN (Generative Adversarial Network)

A type of deep learning model with two neural networks — a **generator** and a **discriminator** — that work against each other. The generator creates data (like images or text), while the discriminator evaluates it for authenticity. This competition helps the model generate highly realistic outputs such as AI-generated art or photos.

General AI (Artificial General Intelligence)

A theoretical form of AI capable of understanding, learning, and applying knowledge across multiple domains — much like a human being. Unlike narrow AI, General AI could perform any intellectual task without specific training.

Genetic Algorithm

An optimization technique inspired by natural selection. It uses processes like mutation, crossover, and selection to evolve solutions to complex problems — often used in robotics, scheduling, and engineering design.

Geospatial AI

The combination of artificial intelligence with geographic data (maps, satellite images, or GPS data) to analyze spatial patterns. It's used in urban planning, agriculture, environmental monitoring, and disaster management.

Gesture Recognition

A branch of computer vision that interprets human movements — such as hand waves or facial expressions — as commands. It's commonly used in gaming, virtual reality, and touchless interfaces.

GPT (Generative Pre-trained Transformer)

A family of large language models developed by OpenAI. GPT models are trained on vast text datasets and can generate human-like text, write essays, code, or answer questions — forming the foundation for conversational AI systems like ChatGPT.

Gradient Descent

An optimization algorithm used in training neural networks. It minimizes the model's prediction error by gradually adjusting weights in the direction of the steepest decrease in loss — similar to rolling downhill to find the lowest point.

Graph Neural Network (GNN)

A type of neural network designed to process data structured as graphs — with nodes (points) and edges (connections). GNNs are used in recommendation systems, molecule analysis, and social network modeling.

Ground Truth

The real, verified data used to measure how accurate an AI model's predictions are. For example, in image recognition, the "ground truth" is the actual label of what the image shows. It's essential for evaluating model performance.

Guided Learning

An AI-assisted educational approach that provides learners with personalized hints, explanations, and progress tracking. Guided learning uses data analytics and adaptive models to support student growth in real time.

🔤 AI Glossary — Letter H

Hallucination (in AI)

A phenomenon where an AI model generates information that appears confident and factual but is actually incorrect or fabricated. Hallucinations occur when the model fills gaps in knowledge or misinterprets data. Managing them requires clear prompts, human review, and fact-checking.

Heuristic Algorithm

A problem-solving method that uses experience-based shortcuts to find good — though not always perfect — solutions quickly. Heuristic algorithms are common in AI search systems, decision-making, and optimization problems where speed matters more than precision.

Hidden Layer

A layer of neurons in a neural network that processes inputs between the input and output layers. Hidden layers extract complex patterns from data and enable the network to make accurate predictions or classifications.

Human-Computer Interaction (HCI)

The study and design of how people interact with computers and AI systems. HCI focuses on usability, accessibility, and user experience, ensuring that AI tools feel intuitive and supportive to human users.

Human-in-the-Loop (HITL)

An AI training or decision process that includes active human participation. Humans review, correct, or guide the AI's outputs to ensure quality, fairness, and ethical alignment — especially important in high-stakes fields like healthcare and law.

Hybrid AI

An approach that combines two or more types of AI — such as symbolic reasoning (rule-based) and machine learning (data-driven) — to create systems that are both interpretable and powerful. Hybrid AI blends logic with learning for smarter, explainable outcomes.

Hyperparameter

A setting or configuration that controls how an AI model learns, such as learning rate, batch size, or number of layers. Unlike model parameters learned automatically, hyperparameters are manually chosen to optimize training performance.

Hyperparameter Tuning

The process of finding the best hyperparameter values for a model. It's often done through techniques like grid search, random search, or Bayesian optimization to achieve the highest accuracy possible.

Hypothesis Testing (in AI)

A statistical method for evaluating whether a pattern or relationship found by an AI model is real or due to chance. It helps ensure that model results are meaningful and scientifically valid.

Hybrid Cloud AI

A cloud computing setup that uses both private and public cloud environments to train and deploy AI models. It offers flexibility, scalability, and stronger control over sensitive data.

🔤 AI Glossary — Letter I

Image Recognition

A branch of computer vision that enables AI systems to identify and categorize objects, people, or scenes in images. It's used in facial recognition, medical imaging, self-driving cars, and quality control in manufacturing.

Imbalanced Data

A situation where some classes or categories in a dataset have many more examples than others. Imbalanced data can cause AI models to favor the majority class, leading to inaccurate predictions. Balancing data improves fairness and performance.

Inference Engine

A component of an AI system that applies logical rules or learned patterns to reach conclusions or make decisions. Inference engines are core parts of expert systems and modern language models that generate intelligent responses.

Information Retrieval

The process of searching, extracting, and ranking relevant data from large datasets or documents. AI-powered search engines and chatbots use information retrieval to deliver accurate, context-aware answers.

Input Data

The raw information — such as text, numbers, or images — that an AI system receives before processing. The quality of input data directly affects the reliability of the model's output.

Intelligent Agent

A software entity capable of perceiving its environment, making decisions, and taking actions to achieve specific goals. Examples include virtual assistants, recommendation systems, and AI tutors.

Interpretable AI

An approach to AI design focused on making model decisions understandable to humans. Interpretable AI helps users trust and verify machine-generated outcomes, especially in healthcare, finance, and law.

Iterative Learning

A process where an AI model improves through repeated cycles of training, testing, and refining. Each iteration helps the system learn from its mistakes and perform better over time.

IoT (Internet of Things) AI

AI integrated with smart devices connected through the internet. IoT AI enables objects like thermostats, watches, and appliances to learn user preferences, predict behavior, and operate autonomously.

Isolation Forest

An anomaly detection algorithm that identifies unusual data points by isolating them from the rest of the dataset. It's efficient for spotting fraud, system errors, or rare events.

🔤 AI Glossary — Letter J

Jaccard Index

A statistical measure used to compare the similarity between two sets. In AI and machine learning, it's often used to evaluate clustering or text similarity by dividing the intersection of sets by their union.

Java (in AI)

A programming language often used in AI applications due to its portability, scalability, and strong memory management. Java supports frameworks like Deeplearning4j and Weka, which help in building AI systems for enterprise and academic use.

Joint Embedding

A technique where two or more types of data — such as text and images — are represented in a shared vector space. Joint embeddings allow AI to link visual and textual understanding, as seen in models like CLIP that connect words to images.

JSON (JavaScript Object Notation)

A lightweight data format used for storing and exchanging structured information between systems. AI tools often use JSON to send model inputs, outputs, and metadata in a clear and readable way.

Jump Learning

An advanced learning concept where AI "jumps ahead" in reasoning or skill based on prior knowledge, instead of learning everything from scratch. It mimics human intuition and helps reduce training time in complex models.

AI Glossary — Letter K

Keyword Extraction

A natural language processing technique used to identify the most relevant words or phrases within text. It helps summarize content, improve search results, and enhance AI-driven document classification.

Kernel Function

A mathematical function used in Support Vector Machines (SVMs) to transform data into a higher-dimensional space. This allows the AI to separate complex, non-linear data more effectively. Common kernel types include linear, polynomial, and radial basis functions.

Kinetic AI

A branch of AI that studies movement and motion analysis. It's used in robotics, sports technology, and autonomous vehicles to understand physical actions and predict motion patterns.

K-Means Clustering

An unsupervised learning algorithm that divides data into *K* distinct groups based on similarity. It assigns each data point to the cluster with the nearest mean value. K-Means is widely used in customer segmentation, image compression, and pattern recognition.

K-Nearest Neighbor (KNN)

A simple yet powerful machine learning algorithm that classifies data based on its proximity to *K* neighboring points. It assumes similar data points are likely to have similar outcomes. KNN is used in recommendation systems and predictive analytics.

Knowledge Base

A structured collection of information that an AI system uses to answer questions, make decisions, or provide explanations. Knowledge bases power systems like virtual assistants, expert systems, and search engines.

Knowledge Distillation

A process where a smaller AI model learns from a larger, more complex model. This helps create faster, lightweight systems that maintain strong performance while using fewer computational resources.

Knowledge Graph

A network that connects information through relationships and context, enabling AI systems to understand how data points relate. Knowledge graphs are used by companies like Google to enhance search accuracy and context understanding.

Knowledge Representation

The method of encoding information in a way that AI systems can understand and use for reasoning. It includes logic rules, ontologies, and semantic networks, allowing AI to store and apply knowledge intelligently.

Knowledge Transfer

A technique in AI and machine learning where knowledge gained from one task or dataset is reused in another. This reduces the need for retraining from scratch and speeds up learning in related areas.

🔤 AI Glossary — Letter L

Label Encoding

A data preprocessing technique used to convert categorical (text-based) values into numerical form so that AI models can process them. For example, "Red," "Green," and "Blue" may be encoded as 0, 1, and 2.

Labeled Data

Data that has been tagged with correct answers or classifications, such as images labeled "cat" or "dog." Labeled data is essential for training supervised learning models that rely on known outcomes.

Language Model

An AI system trained to understand, predict, and generate human language. It learns from massive text datasets to perform tasks like translation, summarization, and conversation — examples include GPT and Gemini.

Latent Space

A hidden mathematical representation within an AI model that captures complex relationships between data points. In generative AI, latent space allows systems to create new images, sounds, or text by exploring abstract features.

Lazy Learning

A machine learning approach where the model delays generalization until a prediction is requested. Algorithms like K-Nearest Neighbor (KNN) store data and only compute results when needed, trading speed for flexibility.

Linear Regression

A basic yet powerful algorithm that predicts outcomes by finding the best-fitting straight line through data points. It's commonly used in finance, sales forecasting, and scientific analysis.

Logistic Regression

A classification algorithm used to predict categorical outcomes (like "yes" or "no") instead of continuous values. Despite its name, it's mainly used for probability-based classification rather than regression.

Long Short-Term Memory (LSTM)

A special type of recurrent neural network (RNN) designed to remember long-term dependencies in sequential data, such as language or time series. LSTMs are used in speech recognition, translation, and text generation.

Loss Function

A mathematical formula that measures how far an AI model's predictions are from the correct answers. The goal of training is to minimize this loss, helping the model improve accuracy over time.

Low-Code AI

AI tools that allow users to build and deploy machine learning models with minimal coding. They simplify development for non-programmers, empowering educators, entrepreneurs, and small businesses to use AI effectively.

🔤 AI Glossary — Letter M

Machine Learning (ML)

A core branch of AI where systems learn from data to make predictions or decisions without being explicitly programmed. It powers tools like recommendation engines, fraud detection, and voice recognition.

Meta Learning

Also called "learning to learn," this technique trains AI systems to adapt quickly to new tasks by using prior knowledge. Meta learning helps models generalize better with less training data.

Model Training

The process of teaching an AI model to recognize patterns by feeding it large amounts of data. During training, the model adjusts its internal parameters to minimize errors and improve predictions.

Model Evaluation

A step where an AI model's accuracy and performance are tested using data it hasn't seen before. Evaluation ensures that the model works well in real-world scenarios.

Model Overfitting

A situation where an AI model learns too closely from training data, capturing noise instead of patterns. Overfitting causes poor performance on new data. Regularization and validation help prevent it.

Model Optimization

The process of improving an AI model's efficiency, accuracy, and speed by fine-tuning its architecture, parameters, or algorithms.

Monte Carlo Simulation

A statistical method that uses random sampling to estimate outcomes in uncertain situations. AI systems use it for risk analysis, forecasting, and game simulations.

Multimodal AI

An AI system capable of understanding and processing information from multiple sources — such as text, images, sound, and video — to produce richer and more accurate results.

Multi-Agent System

A group of AI agents that work together or compete to achieve individual or shared goals. They are used in simulations, logistics, and automated trading systems.

Mutation Algorithm

A process inspired by genetics where random changes are introduced to improve AI models' performance during optimization or evolutionary learning.

🔤 AI Glossary — Letter N

Naive Bayes Algorithm

A simple but powerful machine learning algorithm based on probability. It's widely used in spam detection, text classification, and sentiment analysis.

Named Entity Recognition (NER)

An NLP technique that identifies and classifies specific names or entities (like people, places, or organizations) within text.

Natural Language Processing (NLP)

A field of AI that enables machines to understand and respond to human language. It powers chatbots, translation tools, and voice assistants.

Natural Language Understanding (NLU)

A subset of NLP that focuses on interpreting meaning, emotion, and intent behind text or speech. It allows AI to understand context and tone.

Neural Architecture Search (NAS)

An automated method for designing neural networks. AI systems use NAS to discover optimal model structures without human intervention.

Neural Network

A computational model inspired by the human brain, made of layers of nodes (neurons) that process data. Neural networks are the foundation of deep learning systems.

Neuron

Definition

In artificial intelligence and machine learning, a **neuron** (also called a *node* or *unit*) is the fundamental building block of an artificial neural network. It is modeled loosely after the biological neuron found in the human brain. Each artificial neuron receives input signals, processes them mathematically, and produces an output that is passed to other neurons in the network. Neurons collectively enable a model to learn, recognize patterns, and make predictions by adjusting their internal parameters during training.

Key Components

1. **Inputs:**
   The data values or signals that are fed into the neuron — similar to how biological neurons receive signals through dendrites.
2. **Weights:**
   Numerical values assigned to each input that determine their importance. The neuron learns by adjusting these weights during training.
3. **Summation Function:**
   A mathematical operation that combines the weighted inputs into a single value, often using a simple addition or dot product.
4. **Activation Function:**
   A non-linear function (such as ReLU, Sigmoid, or Tanh) applied to the summation result to decide whether the neuron should "fire" or remain inactive.
5. **Output:**
   The final result produced by the neuron after applying the activation function, which becomes the input for other neurons in subsequent layers.

Benefits

- Allows complex relationships to be learned from raw data.
- Enables non-linear transformations for deep learning tasks.
- Builds scalable and flexible structures that can adapt to various problems.
- Mimics the way biological neurons communicate and adapt over time.

Disadvantages

- Individual neurons are simple and limited in function; meaningful behavior arises only when many are connected.
- May become computationally expensive as the network grows deeper.
- Can overfit data if not properly regularized.

Examples

- A neuron in a **convolutional neural network (CNN)** may detect visual patterns such as edges or textures.
- In a **language model**, neurons may learn linguistic features like word order or meaning.
- In **speech recognition**, neurons can capture tone, pitch, and pronunciation patterns.

Applications

- **Image Recognition:** Detecting and classifying objects, faces, or handwriting.
- **Natural Language Processing:** Understanding text, context, and sentiment.
- **Financial Forecasting:** Identifying market trends from numerical data.
- **Medical Diagnosis:** Interpreting scans, patterns, and patient records.

Industries Using Neuron-Based Models

- **Healthcare:** Predictive diagnosis and imaging analysis.
- **Education:** Adaptive learning and student performance prediction.
- **Technology:** AI assistants, chatbots, and autonomous systems.
- **Transportation:** Self-driving cars and sensor-based navigation.

Challenges

- Understanding neuron-level decision-making remains difficult, leading to "black box" behavior.
- Requires large amounts of data and computational resources to train effectively.
- Sensitive to data quality — poor input can lead to unreliable neuron activation.

Summary

A **neuron** is the core unit of intelligence within an artificial neural network. By processing inputs through weighted connections and activation functions, neurons enable machines to simulate learning and reasoning similar to the human brain. Though individually simple, millions of interconnected neurons together form the foundation of modern AI systems, powering technologies from image recognition to natural language understanding.

Node

A basic unit in a neural network that receives input, processes it, and sends it forward. Nodes collectively form layers that learn from data.

Noise (in Data)

Random or irrelevant information in a dataset that can confuse AI models. Removing noise improves accuracy and training efficiency.

Nonlinear Activation

A mathematical function in neural networks that allows models to learn complex, non-straight-line relationships. Common examples include ReLU, Sigmoid, and Tanh functions.

Normalization

A data preprocessing step that scales values into a consistent range to help AI models learn faster and perform better.

AI Glossary — Letter O

Object Detection

A computer vision technique that identifies and locates objects within an image or video. It's used in autonomous driving, security systems, and retail analytics.

Objective Function

A mathematical formula that defines the goal of an AI model — usually to minimize error or maximize accuracy. It guides the learning process during training.

One-Hot Encoding

A method used to represent categorical data numerically by converting each value into a binary vector. It helps AI systems interpret text-based or labeled inputs.

Ontology (in AI)

A structured framework that defines relationships between concepts within a domain. Ontologies help AI organize knowledge logically and reason effectively.

Optimization Algorithm

A method used to adjust model parameters during training to minimize loss and improve accuracy. Examples include Gradient Descent and Adam Optimizer.

Optimization Problem

A task in AI where the goal is to find the best possible solution — like minimizing cost or maximizing performance — under certain constraints.

Outlier Detection

The process of identifying data points that deviate significantly from the rest. Outlier detection helps find errors, fraud, or anomalies.

Overfitting

When an AI model performs well on training data but fails to generalize to new data because it memorized instead of learning patterns.

Overparameterization

A condition where an AI model has more parameters than necessary, often leading to overfitting and inefficiency.

Oversampling

A data balancing technique that increases the number of examples in an underrepresented class to prevent bias during training.

🔠 AI Glossary — Letter P

Parameter

A value inside an AI model that determines how it makes predictions. Parameters are adjusted during training to minimize error and improve accuracy.

Pattern Recognition

The ability of AI systems to identify regularities, trends, or structures in data. It's used in handwriting recognition, medical imaging, and speech analysis.

Perceptron

One of the earliest types of artificial neural networks. It consists of a single layer of nodes and is used for simple classification tasks.

Predictive Analytics

A branch of AI that uses statistical models and machine learning to forecast future events based on historical data.

Preprocessing

The preparation of data before feeding it into an AI model — including cleaning, scaling, and encoding — to ensure accuracy and consistency.

Probability Distribution

A statistical function that describes the likelihood of different outcomes in a dataset. It's essential for probabilistic reasoning and uncertainty modeling in AI.

Prompt Engineering

The practice of crafting precise and intentional instructions (prompts) to guide AI models in generating accurate and creative responses. It's the foundation of effective human-AI communication.

Probability Distribution

A statistical function that describes the likelihood of different outcomes in a dataset. It's essential for probabilistic reasoning and uncertainty modeling in AI.

Python (Programming Language)

A versatile, easy-to-learn programming language widely used in AI and data science. Python supports major libraries like TensorFlow, PyTorch, and Scikit-learn, making it the most popular tool for AI development.

Pre-trained Model

An AI model that has already been trained on large datasets and can be fine-tuned for specific tasks. Using pre-trained models saves time and computing resources.

Precision and Recall

Two key metrics for evaluating AI performance. **Precision** measures accuracy among positive predictions, while **Recall** measures how many actual positives were correctly identified.

🔠 AI Glossary — Letter Q

Q-Learning

A type of reinforcement learning algorithm where an agent learns to make decisions by receiving rewards or penalties. It helps AI systems determine the best action to take in each situation, such as in robotics or game AI.

Quantization

A technique that reduces the precision of numbers in AI models to make them smaller and faster without major loss in accuracy. It's commonly used to optimize models for mobile or edge devices.

Quantum AI

The integration of quantum computing and artificial intelligence. Quantum AI uses the principles of quantum mechanics to process complex computations faster than traditional computers.

Query

A request for information sent to a database or AI system. In natural language models, queries are user inputs — the "questions" that trigger responses.

Queue Learning

A data-handling strategy where information is processed sequentially, one at a time. It's useful for managing AI tasks or workflows that must follow a specific order.

🔠 AI Glossary — Letter R

Random Forest

An ensemble learning algorithm that combines multiple decision trees to improve accuracy and reduce overfitting. It's used for both classification and regression tasks.

Recurrent Neural Network (RNN)

A neural network designed for sequential data such as text, speech, or time series. RNNs have loops that allow them to "remember" previous inputs, making them ideal for language and forecasting tasks.

Regression Analysis

A statistical method that models the relationship between variables to predict future outcomes. Linear and logistic regression are common types.

Reinforcement Learning

An AI learning method where an agent interacts with its environment and learns from feedback through rewards and penalties. It's used in robotics, gaming, and automation.

Representation Learning

A machine learning technique where the system automatically discovers useful features from raw data instead of relying on manual feature selection.

Retrieval-Augmented Generation (RAG)

A model that combines information retrieval and text generation. It fetches relevant data before producing a response, improving accuracy in AI question-answering systems.

Reward Function

A key component of reinforcement learning that defines how much "reward" an AI receives for taking certain actions. It guides the system toward desirable outcomes.

Robotic Process Automation (RPA)

Technology that uses AI to automate repetitive digital tasks, such as data entry or document processing, to increase efficiency and reduce human error.

Rule-Based System

An AI system that makes decisions based on predefined rules or conditions, often used in expert systems or early AI programs.

Runtime Environment

The system or platform where AI models are executed. It includes the software, hardware, and configurations required for the model to function properly.

🔠 AI Glossary — Letter S

Scalability

The ability of an AI system to handle increasing amounts of data or users without losing performance. Scalable AI models grow with business and computational needs.

Semi-Supervised Learning

A learning method that combines a small amount of labeled data with a large amount of unlabeled data to improve model performance.

Sentiment Analysis

A natural language processing technique that identifies emotions or opinions in text, such as positive, negative, or neutral sentiment. It's used in marketing and social media monitoring.

Signal Processing

The analysis and transformation of data signals (like sound, images, or time series) into meaningful patterns. AI uses it in speech recognition and medical imaging.

Speech Recognition

A technology that converts spoken language into text using AI models trained on voice data. It powers virtual assistants and transcription tools.

Supervised Learning

A machine learning technique where a model is trained using labeled data, meaning both inputs and correct outputs are provided during training.

Swarm Intelligence

An AI concept inspired by nature, where simple agents (like ants or bees) collectively solve complex problems. It's used in optimization, robotics, and network routing.

8. Symbolic AI

An early AI approach based on logical rules and symbolic representations. Unlike modern machine learning, it uses explicit reasoning rather than pattern recognition.

Synthetic Data

Artificially generated data created to train AI models when real data is limited or sensitive. It helps improve privacy and expand datasets.

🔠 AI Glossary — Letter T

Target Variable

The specific outcome or label that an AI model aims to predict, such as "spam or not spam" or "disease present or absent."

TensorFlow

An open-source AI framework developed by Google that helps developers build and train machine learning models efficiently.

Token Limit

The maximum number of tokens (words or symbols) an AI model can process in a single interaction or context window

Tokenization

The process of breaking text into smaller units, or "tokens," such as words or subwords, to help AI models understand language.

Transfer Learning

A technique where a model pre-trained on one task is adapted to a different but related task, saving time and improving performance.

Transformer Architecture

Definition

Transformer Architecture is a deep learning model framework introduced in 2017 by Vaswani et al. in the paper *"Attention Is All You Need."* It revolutionized natural language processing (NLP) by replacing traditional sequence models like RNNs (Recurrent Neural Networks) and LSTMs (Long Short-Term Memory networks) with a mechanism known as **self-attention**, allowing the model to understand relationships between words or elements in a sequence — regardless of their distance from each other.

Key Components

1. **Encoder-Decoder Structure:**
   The architecture typically has two main parts — the encoder, which reads and represents the input data, and the decoder, which generates the output based on the encoded information.
2. **Self-Attention Mechanism:**
   This mechanism lets the model weigh the importance of each word relative to others in a sentence, improving context understanding.
3. **Multi-Head Attention:**
   Multiple attention layers run in parallel, enabling the model to capture different kinds of relationships or meanings simultaneously.
4. **Positional Encoding:**
   Since Transformers do not process data sequentially, positional encodings are added to indicate the order of elements in a sentence.
5. **Feed-Forward Networks:**
   After attention layers, fully connected neural networks help the model transform and refine the contextual representations.
6. **Residual Connections and Layer Normalization:**
   These ensure stability during training and help the model learn complex patterns efficiently.

Benefits

- Handles long-range dependencies more effectively than RNNs.
- Enables parallel processing, making it faster to train on large datasets.

- Produces state-of-the-art performance across multiple tasks, such as translation, summarization, and text generation.
- Scales well to massive datasets and larger models like GPT, BERT, and T5.

Disadvantages

- Extremely data- and computation-intensive, requiring powerful hardware.
- Can be prone to bias if trained on unbalanced or low-quality datasets.
- Difficult to interpret because of its complexity and multi-layered attention mechanisms.

Applications

- **Natural Language Processing (NLP):** Machine translation, text summarization, sentiment analysis, and chatbots.
- **Vision Transformers (ViTs):** Image recognition and object detection in computer vision.
- **Speech Recognition:** Improved context-aware transcription and voice command systems.
- **Multimodal AI:** Combining text, images, and audio for generative and reasoning tasks.

Industries Using Transformer Models

- **Technology:** Google, OpenAI, Meta, and Microsoft for large-scale AI systems.
- **Education:** Intelligent tutoring systems and adaptive learning platforms.
- **Healthcare:** Medical data analysis and clinical text interpretation.
- **Entertainment:** Script generation, gaming narratives, and subtitles translation.

Challenges

- High energy consumption during training and inference.
- Potential for producing inaccurate or biased outputs if the model is not fine-tuned properly.
- Data privacy concerns in large-scale, open-domain training environments.

Summary

The Transformer Architecture represents a fundamental shift in how machines understand and generate language. Its self-attention mechanism allows models to process context more globally and flexibly than ever before. Transformers laid the foundation for today's most advanced AI systems — including ChatGPT, BERT, and countless others — marking a turning point in modern artificial intelligence.

Transformer Model

A neural network architecture that processes sequences of data (like text) more efficiently than traditional RNNs. It's the foundation of modern large language models such as GPT.

Training Data

The dataset used to teach an AI model. Training data must be diverse and accurate to ensure reliable model performance.

Turing Test

A test developed by Alan Turing to evaluate whether a machine can exhibit intelligent behavior indistinguishable from that of a human.

Time Series Analysis

The use of AI to analyze sequential data over time, such as stock prices or weather patterns, to forecast future trends.

Tunable Parameters

Adjustable values in an AI model that influence its performance, such as learning rate or layer depth. Tuning helps achieve optimal results.

AI Glossary — Letter U

Unlabeled Data

Data that has not been tagged with specific outputs or categories. It's commonly used in unsupervised and semi-supervised learning.

Unstructured Data

Information that doesn't follow a predefined format, such as text, images, videos, or social media posts. AI tools process it using natural language and computer vision techniques.

Unsupervised Learning

A machine learning method where models learn from unlabeled data to find patterns, groupings, or hidden structures without specific instructions.

Uncertainty Modeling

The process of estimating how confident an AI model is about its predictions. It helps improve trust and decision-making in sensitive domains like medicine or finance.

Update Rate

The frequency at which an AI model adjusts its parameters during training. A balanced update rate ensures faster learning without instability.

User Intent Recognition

An NLP technique that determines the purpose or goal behind a user's input — essential in chatbots and voice assistants for accurate responses.

Utility Function

A mathematical function used in AI to evaluate the desirability or usefulness of different actions. It's often used in decision-making and reinforcement learning.

🔠 AI Glossary — Letter V

Validation Set

A portion of the dataset used during model training to fine-tune parameters and prevent overfitting. It helps evaluate how well the model generalizes to unseen data before final testing.

Value Function (in Reinforcement Learning)

A function that estimates the expected reward an AI agent will receive from a certain state or action. It guides decision-making by helping the agent choose actions that maximize long-term rewards.

Variance (in AI Models)

A measure of how much a model's predictions change when trained on different data samples. High variance means the model is sensitive to noise and may overfit.

Vectorization

The process of converting data (like text or images) into numerical vectors that AI models can process. It's essential in natural language processing and computer vision.

Verification (in AI Systems)

The process of checking whether an AI model or system performs its intended function correctly and safely before deployment.

Virtual Agent

An AI-driven digital assistant designed to interact with humans through voice or text. Examples include chatbots, customer service bots, and AI tutors.

Virtual Reality (VR)

A computer-generated environment that simulates real or imagined worlds. When combined with AI, VR can create adaptive, interactive learning and training experiences.

Vision Transformer (ViT)

A deep learning model that applies transformer architecture — originally used for language — to image recognition tasks. It divides images into patches and processes them like words in a sentence.

Voice Recognition

AI technology that identifies and processes human voices to perform tasks, such as unlocking devices or activating voice assistants.

Volumetric Data

Three-dimensional data used in fields like medical imaging, 3D modeling, and geoscience. AI uses it to analyze structures and visualize depth in complex environments.

AI Glossary — Letter W

Weak AI (Narrow AI)

AI designed to perform a specific task, such as translation or image classification. It does not possess general reasoning or consciousness like humans.

Weight (in Neural Networks)

A numerical value that determines the strength of a connection between neurons. During training, weights are adjusted to reduce prediction errors.

Weighted Average

A statistical method that assigns different importance (weights) to data points when calculating an average. AI uses it to prioritize more relevant or reliable data.

Whisper Model

An AI model developed by OpenAI for automatic speech recognition (ASR). It transcribes and translates spoken language into text across multiple languages with high accuracy.

Wi-Fi Sensing AI

Technology that uses Wi-Fi signals to detect movement or monitor environments without cameras. It's used in security, healthcare, and smart homes.

Windowing Function

A mathematical function used in signal processing and speech recognition to divide data into smaller segments for analysis.

Word Embedding

A representation of words in numerical form where similar words are placed close together in vector space. It helps AI models understand semantic relationships in text.

Word2Vec

A popular algorithm for creating word embeddings by learning relationships between words based on their context within large text datasets.

Workflow Automation

The use of AI to streamline repetitive business tasks such as approvals, document sorting, and scheduling. It increases productivity and reduces human error.

World Model (in AI)

A conceptual model an AI system builds to understand and predict the behavior of the environment around it — especially in robotics and autonomous systems.

🔠 AI Glossary — Letter X

XAI (Explainable AI)

A field of AI focused on making models transparent and understandable to humans. It explains how decisions are made, which builds trust and accountability.

XGBoost (Extreme Gradient Boosting)

A powerful machine learning algorithm known for its high performance in classification and regression tasks. It's widely used in data science competitions and predictive modeling.

XML (Extensible Markup Language)

A structured text format used to store and share data between systems. AI applications use XML for configuration, annotations, and data exchange.

XOR Problem

A classic logic problem that early neural networks struggled to solve. It led to the development of multilayer neural networks capable of learning non-linear relationships.

🔠 AI Glossary — Letter Y

YAML (YAML Ain't Markup Language)

A human-readable data format often used for AI configuration files, datasets, and machine learning pipelines. It's easy to read and integrates well with Python-based AI frameworks.

Yield Prediction AI

AI systems that forecast agricultural output based on environmental data, crop type, and soil conditions. It supports smarter farming and food sustainability.

Yearly Seasonality Model

A model used in time-series forecasting that accounts for repeating annual patterns — such as sales spikes or weather cycles — to improve accuracy.

YOLO (You Only Look Once)

A fast real-time object detection algorithm that identifies and locates multiple objects in a single pass. It's widely used in autonomous vehicles and security systems.

🔠 AI Glossary — Letter Z

Zero-Shot Learning

An AI method that allows a model to recognize new objects or tasks it has never seen before by using prior knowledge or contextual reasoning.

Zettabyte

A unit of digital storage equal to one sextillion (10^{21}) bytes. AI models and data centers increasingly operate with zettabyte-scale data due to massive global information growth.

Z-Score Normalization

A statistical technique used to standardize data by subtracting the mean and dividing by the standard deviation. It helps machine learning models handle data with different scales.

Zone-Based AI

A decision-making approach where an AI system divides its environment into regions or "zones" for localized reasoning and optimized control — used in robotics and traffic management.

Zoom Out Learning

A training strategy where AI is encouraged to look at problems from broader perspectives rather than narrow details, improving reasoning and generalization.

💥 Epilogue

When I began this journey, I didn't set out to write a complicated programming book.
I wanted to create a guide that **takes away the fear of coding** — a handbook that reminds

you that learning technology doesn't have to be overwhelming or technical. It can be **simple, creative, and rewarding**, one small snippet at a time.

Each snippet in this book is more than just a piece of code — it's a tiny bridge between imagination and creation.
Maybe you used one to fix a button on your WordPress site, another to display the current year automatically, or perhaps one that embedded your first chatbot.
No matter how small it may seem, that snippet represents something big: **progress.**

Technology evolves fast, but the mindset behind it never changes — curiosity, patience, and courage.
You've now learned that a few lines of code can transform a blank page into a living, breathing idea.
You've seen how reusability makes work smarter, not harder.
And you've proven to yourself that **you can build something valuable with what you already have** — your willingness to learn.

As you continue your journey, I hope you'll keep exploring and collecting your own snippets — those small treasures that make digital creation easier and more personal.
You don't have to memorize every line; you just need to understand what each piece does, and how it connects to something greater.

If there's one thing I hope you take from this book, it's this:

You don't have to be a programmer to think like one.
You just need curiosity, creativity, and the courage to start.

So go ahead — build your next website, automate your next task, or design your next AI project.
Keep learning, keep experimenting, and remember that every great system, website, or idea begins with a simple snippet.

Thank you for letting me be part of your journey into coding with confidence and simplicity.
And remember — technology isn't just about what you code.
It's about what you create, who you help, and how you grow along the way.

— *Susie Hala*

INDEX

The Snippet Handbook: Reusable Code for Beginners

KO E 'OTUA MO TONGA KO HOKU TOFI'A
TONGA

alamy

www.ingramcontent.com/pod-product-compliance
Lightning Source LLC
LaVergne TN
LVHW070910210926
848482LV00017B/1037